WHO FRAMEWORK CONVENTION ON TOBACCO CONTROL

Guidelines for implementation

Article 5.3; Article 8; Article 11; Article 13

WHO Library Cataloguing-in-Publication Data :

WHO Framework Convention on Tobacco Control : guidelines for implementation Article 5.3; Article 8; Article 11; Article 13.

1.Tobacco industry - legislation. 2.Smoking - adverse effects. 3.Smoking - legislation. 4.Tobacco-derived products labelling. 5.Tobacco control campaigns. I.World Health Organization.

ISBN 978 92 4 159822 4   (NLM classification: HD 9130.6)

TABLE OF CONTENTS

**GUIDELINES FOR IMPLEMENTATION OF ARTICLE 5.3
OF THE WHO FRAMEWORK CONVENTION ON TOBACCO CONTROL**

*Protection of public health policies with respect to tobacco control
from commercial and other vested interests of the tobacco industry* 1

**GUIDELINES FOR IMPLEMENTATION OF ARTICLE 8
OF THE WHO FRAMEWORK CONVENTION ON TOBACCO CONTROL**

Protection from exposure to tobacco smoke 17

**GUIDELINES FOR IMPLEMENTATION OF ARTICLE 11
OF THE WHO FRAMEWORK CONVENTION ON TOBACCO CONTROL**

Packaging and labelling of tobacco products 31

**GUIDELINES FOR IMPLEMENTATION OF ARTICLE 13
OF THE WHO FRAMEWORK CONVENTION ON TOBACCO CONTROL**

Tobacco advertising, promotion and sponsorship 49

FOREWORD

This publication contains the first set of guidelines adopted by the Conference of the Parties at its Second (2007) and Third (2008) sessions. These four guidelines cover a wide range of provisions of the WHO Framework Convention on Tobacco Control, such as: the protection of public health policies with respect to tobacco control from commercial and other vested interests of the tobacco industry (Article 5.3); protection from exposure to tobacco smoke (Article 8); packaging and labelling of tobacco products (Article 11); and tobacco advertising, promotion and sponsorship (Article 13). The publication has been prepared by the Convention Secretariat in order to promote implementation of the Framework Convention.

The guidelines are intended to help Parties to meet their obligations under the respective provisions of the Convention. They reflect the consolidated views of Parties on different aspects of implementation, their experiences and achievements, and the challenges faced. The guidelines also aim to reflect and promote best practices and standards that governments would benefit from in the treaty-implementation process.

Guidelines on other articles of the Convention are currently being prepared by intergovernmental working groups and will be submitted to the Conference of the Parties for consideration at its future sessions.

The guidelines were prepared through the work of representatives of the Parties in the intergovernmental working groups established by the Conference of the Parties, with further input from Parties during the commentary process and the discussions at the Conference of the Parties, intergovernmental and nongovernmental organizations accredited as observers to the Conference, and invited experts.

As a result of this wide consultative process and the consensus reached by the Parties, the guidelines have become widely acknowledged as a valuable tool in the implementation of the Framework Convention.

Dr Haik Nikogosian
Head of the Convention Secretariat

Guidelines for implementation
Article 5.3

GUIDELINES FOR IMPLEMENTATION OF ARTICLE 5.3 OF THE WHO FRAMEWORK CONVENTION ON TOBACCO CONTROL

PROTECTION OF PUBLIC HEALTH POLICIES WITH RESPECT TO TOBACCO CONTROL FROM COMMERCIAL AND OTHER VESTED INTERESTS OF THE TOBACCO INDUSTRY

INTRODUCTION

World Health Assembly resolution WHA54.18 on transparency in tobacco control process, citing the findings of the Committee of Experts on Tobacco Industry Documents, states that "the tobacco industry has operated for years with the express intention of subverting the role of governments and of WHO in implementing public health policies to combat the tobacco epidemic".

The Preamble of the WHO Framework Convention on Tobacco Control recognized the Parties'[1] "need to be alert to any efforts by the tobacco industry to undermine or subvert tobacco control efforts and the need to be informed of activities of the tobacco industry that have a negative impact on tobacco control efforts".

Further, Article 5.3 of the Convention requires that "in setting and implementing their public health policies with respect to tobacco control, Parties shall act to protect these policies from commercial and other vested interests of the tobacco industry in accordance with national law".

The Conference of the Parties, in decision FCTC/COP2(14), established a working group to elaborate guidelines for implementation of Article 5.3 of the Convention.

Without prejudice to the sovereign right of the Parties to determine and establish their tobacco control policies, Parties are encouraged to implement these guidelines to the extent possible in accordance with their national law.

Purpose, scope and applicability

Use of the guidelines for implementation of Article 5.3 of the Convention will have an overarching impact on countries' tobacco control policies and on implementation of the Convention, because the guidelines recognize that

---

[1] "The term 'Parties' refers to States and other entities with treaty-making capacity which have expressed their consent to be bound by a treaty and where the treaty is in force for such States and entities." (Source: United Nations Treaty Collections: http://untreaty.un.org/English/guide.asp#signatories).

tobacco industry interference, including that from the State-owned tobacco industry, cuts across a number of tobacco control policy areas, as stated in the Preamble of the Convention, articles referring to specific tobacco control policies and the Rules of Procedure of the Conference of the Parties to the WHO Framework Convention on Tobacco Control.

The purpose of these guidelines is to ensure that efforts to protect tobacco control from commercial and other vested interests of the tobacco industry are comprehensive and effective. Parties should implement measures in all branches of government that may have an interest in, or the capacity to, affect public health policies with respect to tobacco control.

The aim of these guidelines is to assist Parties[2] in meeting their legal obligations under Article 5.3 of the Convention. The guidelines draw on the best available scientific evidence and the experience of Parties in addressing tobacco industry interference.

The guidelines apply to setting and implementing Parties' public health policies with respect to tobacco control. They also apply to persons, bodies or entities that contribute to, or could contribute to, the formulation, implementation, administration or enforcement of those policies.

The guidelines are applicable to government officials, representatives and employees of any national, state, provincial, municipal, local or other public or semi/quasi-public institution or body within the jurisdiction of a Party, and to any person acting on their behalf. Any government branch (executive, legislative and judiciary) responsible for setting and implementing tobacco control policies and for protecting those policies against tobacco industry interests should be accountable.

The broad array of strategies and tactics used by the tobacco industry to interfere with the setting and implementing of tobacco control measures, such as those that Parties to the Convention are required to implement, is documented by a vast body of evidence. The measures recommended in these guidelines aim at protecting against interference not only by the tobacco industry but also, as appropriate, by organizations and individuals that work to further the interests of the tobacco industry.

While the measures recommended in these guidelines should be applied by Parties as broadly as necessary, in order best to achieve the objectives of Article 5.3 of the Convention, Parties are strongly urged to implement measures beyond those recommended in these guidelines when adapting them to their specific circumstances.

---

[2] Where appropriate, these guidelines also refer to regional economic integration organizations.

GUIDING PRINCIPLES

Principle 1: There is a fundamental and irreconcilable conflict between the tobacco industry's interests and public health policy interests.

The tobacco industry produces and promotes a product that has been proven scientifically to be addictive, to cause disease and death and to give rise to a variety of social ills, including increased poverty. Therefore, Parties should protect the formulation and implementation of public health policies for tobacco control from the tobacco industry to the greatest extent possible.

Principle 2: Parties, when dealing with the tobacco industry or those working to further its interests, should be accountable and transparent.

Parties should ensure that any interaction with the tobacco industry on matters related to tobacco control or public health is accountable and transparent.

Principle 3: Parties should require the tobacco industry and those working to further its interests to operate and act in a manner that is accountable and transparent.

The tobacco industry should be required to provide Parties with information for effective implementation of these guidelines.

Principle 4: Because their products are lethal, the tobacco industry should not be granted incentives to establish or run their businesses.

Any preferential treatment of the tobacco industry would be in conflict with tobacco control policy.

RECOMMENDATIONS

The following important activities are recommended for addressing tobacco industry interference in public health policies:

(1) Raise awareness about the addictive and harmful nature of tobacco products and about tobacco industry interference with Parties' tobacco control policies.

(2) Establish measures to limit interactions with the tobacco industry and ensure the transparency of those interactions that occur.

(3) Reject partnerships and non-binding or non-enforceable agreements with the tobacco industry.

(4) Avoid conflicts of interest for government officials and employees.

(5) Require that information provided by the tobacco industry be transparent and accurate

(6) Denormalize and, to the extent possible, regulate activities described as "socially responsible" by the tobacco industry, including but not limited to activities described as "corporate social responsibility".

(7) Do not give preferential treatment to the tobacco industry.

(8) Treat State-owned tobacco industry in the same way as any other tobacco industry.

Agreed measures for protecting public health policies with respect to tobacco control from commercial and other vested interests of the tobacco industry are listed below. Parties are encouraged to implement measures beyond those provided for by these guidelines, and nothing in these guidelines shall prevent a Party from imposing stricter requirements that are consistent with these recommendations.

(1) Raise awareness about the addictive and harmful nature of tobacco products and about tobacco industry interference with Parties' tobacco control policies.

All branches of government and the public need knowledge and awareness about past and present interference by the tobacco industry in setting and implementing public health policies with respect to tobacco control. Such interference requires specific action for successful implementation of the whole Framework Convention.

Recommendations

1.1 Parties should, in consideration of Article 12 of the Convention, inform and educate all branches of government and the public about the addictive and harmful nature of tobacco products, the need to protect public health policies for tobacco control from commercial and other vested interests of the tobacco industry and the strategies and tactics used by the tobacco industry to interfere with the setting and implementation of public health policies with respect to tobacco control.

1.2 Parties should, in addition, raise awareness about the tobacco industry's practice of using individuals, front groups and affiliated organizations to act, openly or covertly, on their behalf or to take action to further the interests of the tobacco industry.

(2) Establish measures to limit interactions with the tobacco industry and ensure the transparency of those interactions that occur.

In setting and implementing public health policies with respect to tobacco control, any necessary interaction with the tobacco industry should be carried out by Parties in such a way as to avoid the creation of any perception of a real or potential partnership or cooperation resulting from or on account of such interaction. In the event the tobacco industry engages in any conduct that may create such a perception, Parties should act to prevent or correct this perception.

Recommendations

2.1 Parties should interact with the tobacco industry only when and to the extent strictly necessary to enable them to effectively regulate the tobacco industry and tobacco products.

2.2 Where interactions with the tobacco industry are necessary, Parties should ensure that such interactions are conducted transparently. Whenever possible, interactions should be conducted in public, for example through public hearings, public notice of interactions, disclosure of records of such interactions to the public.

(3) Reject partnerships and non-binding or non-enforceable agreements with the tobacco industry.

The tobacco industry should not be a partner in any initiative linked to setting or implementing public health policies, given that its interests are in direct conflict with the goals of public health.

Recommendations

3.1 Parties should not accept, support or endorse partnerships and non-binding or non-enforceable agreements as well as any voluntary arrangement with the tobacco industry or any entity or person working to further its interests.

3.2 Parties should not accept, support or endorse the tobacco industry organizing, promoting, participating in, or performing, youth, public education or any initiatives that are directly or indirectly related to tobacco control.

3.3 Parties should not accept, support or endorse any voluntary code of conduct or instrument drafted by the tobacco industry that is offered as a substitute for legally enforceable tobacco control measures.

3.4 Parties should not accept, support or endorse any offer for assistance or proposed tobacco control legislation or policy drafted by or in collaboration with the tobacco industry.

(4) Avoid conflicts of interest for government officials and employees.

The involvement of organizations or individuals with commercial or vested interests in the tobacco industry in public health policies with respect to tobacco control is most likely to have a negative effect. Clear rules regarding conflicts of interest for government officials and employees working in tobacco control are important means for protecting such policies from interference by the tobacco industry.

Payments, gifts and services, monetary or in-kind, and research funding offered by the tobacco industry to government institutions, officials or employees can create conflicts of interest. Conflicting interests are created even if a promise of favourable consideration is not given in exchange, as the potential exists for personal interest to influence official responsibilities as recognized in the International Code of Conduct for Public Officials adopted by the United Nations General Assembly and by several governmental and regional economic integration organizations.

Recommendations

4.1 Parties should mandate a policy on the disclosure and management of conflicts of interest that applies to all persons involved in setting and implementing public health policies with respect to tobacco control, including government officials, employees, consultants and contractors.

4.2 Parties should formulate, adopt and implement a code of conduct for public officials, prescribing the standards with which they should comply in their dealings with the tobacco industry.

4.3 Parties should not award contracts for carrying out any work related to setting and implementing public health policies with respect to tobacco control to candidates or tenderers who have conflicts of interest with established tobacco control policies.

4.4 Parties should develop clear policies that require public office holders who have or have had a role in setting and implementing public health policies with respect to tobacco control to inform their institutions about any intention to engage in an occupational activity within the tobacco industry, whether gainful or not, within a specified period of time after leaving service.

4.5 Parties should develop clear policies that require applicants for public office positions which have a role in setting and implementing public health policies with respect to tobacco control to declare any current or previous occupational activity with any tobacco industry whether gainful or not.

4.6 Parties should require government officials to declare and divest themselves of direct interests in the tobacco industry.

4.7 Government institutions and their bodies should not have any financial interest in the tobacco industry, unless they are responsible for managing a Party's ownership interest in a State-owned tobacco industry.

4.8 Parties should not allow any person employed by the tobacco industry or any entity working to further its interests to be a member of any government body, committee or advisory group that sets or implements tobacco control or public health policy.

4.9 Parties should not nominate any person employed by the tobacco industry or any entity working to further its interests to serve on delegations to meetings of the Conference of the Parties, its subsidiary bodies or any other bodies established pursuant to decisions of the Conference of the Parties.

4.10 Parties should not allow any official or employee of government or of any semi/quasi-governmental body to accept payments, gifts or services, monetary or in-kind, from the tobacco industry.

4.11 Taking into account national law and constitutional principles, Parties should have effective measures to prohibit contributions from the tobacco industry or any entity working to further its interests to political parties, candidates or campaigns, or to require full disclosure of such contributions.

(5) Require that information provided by the tobacco industry be transparent and accurate.

To take effective measures preventing interference of the tobacco industry with public health policies, Parties need information about its activities and practices, thus ensuring that the industry operates in a transparent manner. Article 12 of the Convention requires Parties to promote public access to such information in accordance with national law.

Article 20.4 of the Convention requires, inter alia, Parties to promote and facilitate exchanges of information about tobacco industry practices and the cultivation of tobacco. In accordance with Article 20.4(c) of the Convention, each Party should endeavour to cooperate with competent international organizations to establish progressively and maintain a global system to regularly collect and disseminate information on tobacco production and manufacture and activities of the tobacco industry which have an impact on the Convention or national tobacco control activities.

Recommendations

5.1 Parties should introduce and apply measures to ensure that all operations and activities of the tobacco industry are transparent.[3]

5.2 Parties should require the tobacco industry and those working to further its interests to periodically submit information on tobacco production, manufacture, market share, marketing expenditures, revenues and any other activity, including lobbying, philanthropy, political contributions and all other activities not prohibited or not yet prohibited under Article 13 of the Convention.[3]

5.3 Parties should require rules for the disclosure or registration of the tobacco industry entities, affiliated organizations and individuals acting on their behalf, including lobbyists.

5.4 Parties should impose mandatory penalties on the tobacco industry in case of the provision of false or misleading information in accordance with national law.

5.5 Parties should adopt and implement effective legislative, executive, administrative and other measures to ensure public access, in accordance with Article 12(c) of the Convention, to a wide range of information on tobacco industry activities as relevant to the objectives of the Convention, such as in a public repository.

(6) Denormalize and, to the extent possible, regulate activities described as "socially responsible" by the tobacco industry, including but not limited to activities described as "corporate social responsibility".

The tobacco industry conducts activities described as socially responsible to distance its image from the lethal nature of the product it produces and sells or to interfere with the setting and implementation of public health policies. Activities that are described as "socially responsible" by the tobacco industry, aiming at the promotion of tobacco consumption, is a marketing as well as a public relations strategy that falls within the Convention's definition of advertising, promotion and sponsorship.

The corporate social responsibility of the tobacco industry is, according to WHO,[4] an inherent contradiction, as industry's core functions are in conflict with the goals of public health policies with respect to tobacco control.

Recommendations

6.1 Parties should ensure that all branches of government and the public are informed and made aware of the true purpose and

---

[3] Without prejudice to trade secrets or confidential information protected by law.

[4] WHO. *Tobacco industry and corporate social responsibility – an inherent contradiction.* Geneva, World Health Organization, 2004.

scope of activities described as socially responsible performed by the tobacco industry.

6.2 Parties should not endorse, support, form partnerships with or participate in activities of the tobacco industry described as socially responsible.

6.3 Parties should not allow public disclosure by the tobacco industry or any other person acting on its behalf of activities described as socially responsible or of the expenditures made for these activities, except when legally required to report on such expenditures, such as in an annual report.[5]

6.4 Parties should not allow acceptance by any branch of government or the public sector of political, social, financial, educational, community or other contributions from the tobacco industry or from those working to further its interests, except for compensations due to legal settlements or mandated by law or legally binding and enforceable agreements.

(7) Do not give preferential treatment to the tobacco industry.

Some governments encourage investments by the tobacco industry, even to the extent of subsidizing them with financial incentives, such as providing partial or complete exemption from taxes otherwise mandated by law.

Without prejudice to their sovereign right to determine and establish their economic, financial and taxation policies, Parties should respect their commitments for tobacco control.

Recommendations

7.1 Parties should not grant incentives, privileges or benefits to the tobacco industry to establish or run their businesses.

7.2 Parties that do not have a State-owned tobacco industry should not invest in the tobacco industry and related ventures. Parties with a State-owned tobacco industry should ensure that any investment in the tobacco industry does not prevent them from fully implementing the WHO Framework Convention on Tobacco Control.

7.3 Parties should not provide any preferential tax exemption to the tobacco industry.

---

[5] The guidelines for implementation of Article 13 of the WHO Framework Convention on Tobacco Control address this subject from the perspective of tobacco advertising, promotion and sponsorship.

(8) Treat State-owned tobacco industry in the same way as any other tobacco industry.

Tobacco industry can be government-owned, non-government-owned or a combination thereof. These guidelines apply to all tobacco industry, regardless of its ownership.

Recommendations

8.1   Parties should ensure that State-owned tobacco industry is treated in the same way as any other member of the tobacco industry in respect of setting and implementing tobacco control policy.

8.2   Parties should ensure that the setting and implementing of tobacco control policy are separated from overseeing or managing tobacco industry.

8.3   Parties should ensure that representatives of State-owned tobacco industry does not form part of delegations to any meetings of the Conference of the Parties, its subsidiary bodies or any other bodies established pursuant to decisions of the Conference of the Parties.

ENFORCEMENT AND MONITORING

Enforcement

Parties should put in place enforcement mechanisms or, to the extent possible, use existing enforcement mechanisms to meet their obligations under Article 5.3 of the Convention and these guidelines.

Monitoring implementation of Article 5.3 of the Convention and of these guidelines

Monitoring implementation of Article 5.3 of the Convention and of these guidelines is essential for ensuring the introduction and implementation of efficient tobacco control policies. This should also involve monitoring the tobacco industry, for which existing models and resources should be used, such as the database on tobacco industry monitoring of the WHO Tobacco Free Initiative.

Nongovernmental organizations and other members of civil society not affiliated with the tobacco industry could play an essential role in monitoring the activities of the tobacco industry.

Codes of conduct or staff regulations for all branches of governments should include a "whistleblower function", with adequate protection of whistleblowers.

In addition, Parties should be encouraged to use and enforce mechanisms to ensure compliance with these guidelines, such as the possibility of bringing an action to court, and to use complaint procedures such as an ombudsman system.

INTERNATIONAL COLLABORATION AND UPDATING AND REVISION OF THE GUIDELINES

International cooperation is essential for making progress in preventing interference by the tobacco industry with the formulation of public health policies on tobacco control. Article 20.4 of the Convention provides the basis for collecting and exchanging knowledge and experience with respect to tobacco industry practices, taking into account and addressing the special needs of developing country Parties and Parties with economies in transition.

Efforts have already been made to coordinate the collection and dissemination of national and international experience with regard to the strategies and tactics used by the tobacco industry and to the monitoring of tobacco industry activities. Parties would benefit from sharing legal and strategic expertise for countering tobacco industry strategies. Article 21.4 of the Convention provides that information exchange should be subject to national laws regarding confidentiality and privacy.

Recommendations

As the strategies and tactics used by the tobacco industry evolve constantly, these guidelines should be reviewed and revised periodically to ensure that they continue to provide effective guidance to Parties on protecting their public health policies on tobacco control from tobacco industry interference.

Parties reporting via the existing reporting instrument of the Framework Convention should provide information on tobacco production and manufacture and the activities of the tobacco industry that affect the Convention or national tobacco control activities. To facilitate this exchange, the Convention Secretariat should ensure that the principal provisions of these guidelines are reflected in the next phases of the reporting instrument, which the Conference of the Parties will gradually adopt for use by Parties.

In view of the paramount importance of preventing tobacco industry interference in any public health policy with respect to tobacco control, the Conference of the Parties may, in the light of experience with implementing these guidelines, consider whether there is a need to elaborate a protocol in relation to Article 5.3 of the Convention.

USEFUL SOURCES OF INFORMATION

Relevant literature

Brandt AM. *The cigarette century. The rise, fall, and deadly persistence of the product that defined America*. New York, Basic Books, 2007.

Chapman S. *Making smoking history. Public health advocacy and tobacco control*. Oxford, Blackwell Publishing, 2007.

Callard C, Thompson D, Collishaw N. *Curing the addiction to profits: a supply-side approach to phasing out tobacco*. Ottawa, Canadian Centre for Policy Alternatives and Physicians for a Smoke free Canada, 2005.

Feldman EA, Bayer R (Editors). *Unfiltered: conflicts over tobacco policy and public health*. Boston, Harvard University Press, 2004.

Gilmore A et al. Continuing influence of tobacco industry in Germany. *Lancet*, 2002, 360:1255.

Hastings G, Angus K. *The influence of the tobacco industry on European tobacco control policy. In: Tobacco or health in the European Union. Past, present and future*. Luxembourg, Office for Official Publications of the European Commission, 2004:195–225.

Lavack A. *Tobacco industry denormalization campaigns: a review and evaluation*. Ottawa, Health Canada, 2001.

Mahood G. *Tobacco industry denormalization. Telling the truth about the tobacco industry's role in the tobacco epidemic*. Toronto, Campaign for Tobacco Industry Denormalization, 2004.

Pan American Health Organization. *Profits over people. Tobacco industry activities to market cigarettes and undermine public health in Latin America and the Caribbean*. Washington DC, Pan American Health Organization, 2002.

Simpson D. Germany: still sleeping with the enemy. *Tobacco Control*, 2003, 12:343–344.

Hammond R, Rowell A. *Trust us. We're the tobacco industry*. Baltimore, Johns Hopkins University Press, 2001.

World Health Organization. *Tobacco company strategies to undermine tobacco control activities at the World Health Organization*. Geneva, World Health Organization, 2000.

World Health Organization. *Tobacco industry and corporate social responsibility – an inherent contradiction*. Geneva, World Health Organization, 2004.

Yach D, Bialous S. Junking science to promote tobacco. *American Journal of Public Health*, 2001, 91:1745–1748.

Web resources

WHO sites:
Tobacco Free Initiative: http://www.who.int/tobacco/en/

WHO publications on tobacco:
http://www.who.int/tobacco/resources/publications/en/

WHO European Regional Office:
http://www.euro.who.int/healthtopics/HT2ndLvlPage?HTCode=smoking

Tobacco control in the Americas (in English and Spanish):
http://www.paho.org/english/ad/sde/ra/Tobabout.htm

Sites with general, regional or national information and topics related to tobacco control:
Action on Smoking and Health, UK (and special page for the tobacco industry):
http://www.newash.org.uk/ash_r3iitasl.htm

Corporate Accountability International and the Network for Accountability of Tobacco Transnationals: www.stopcorporateabuse.org

Economics of tobacco control: http://www1.worldbank.org/tobacco/

European Commission:
http://ec.europa.eu/health/ph_determinants/life_style/Tobacco/tobacco_en.htm

European Network for Smoking Prevention: http://www.ensp.org/

Framework Convention Alliance for Tobacco Control: http://www.fctc.org/

International Union for Health Promotion and Education:
http://www.iuhpe.org/?page=18&lang=en

Model Legislation for Tobacco Control manual:
http://www.iuhpe.org/?lang=en&page=publications_report2

Tobacco industry:
http://tobacco.health.usyd.edu.au/site/supersite/links/docs/tobacco_ind.htm

Smokefree Partnership: http://www.smokefreepartnership.eu/

Thailand Health Promotion Institute: http://www.thpinhf.org/

Tobaccopedia: the online tobacco encyclopaedia: http://www.tobaccopedia.org/

More links to tobacco sites:

Various international and national tobacco control web sites:
http://www.tobacco.org/resources/general/tobsites.html

National tobacco control web sites:
http://www.smokefreepartnership.eu/National-Tobacco-Control-websites

Centre de ressources anti-tabac: http://www.tabac-info.net/

Comité National Contre le Tabagisme (France): http://www.cnct.org

Office Français de Prévention du Tabagisme: http://www.oft-asso.fr/

Latest news on smoking and tobacco control: http://www.globalink.org

Ministère de la santé, de la jeunesse et des sports: http://www.sante.gouv.fr/

Guidelines for implementation
Article 8

GUIDELINES FOR IMPLEMENTATION OF ARTICLE 8 OF THE WHO FRAMEWORK CONVENTION ON TOBACCO CONTROL

PROTECTION FROM EXPOSURE TO TOBACCO SMOKE

PURPOSE, OBJECTIVES AND KEY CONSIDERATIONS

Purpose of the guidelines

Consistent with other provisions of the WHO Framework Convention on Tobacco Control and the intentions of the Conference of the Parties, these guidelines are intended to assist Parties in meeting their obligations under Article 8 of the Convention. They draw on the best available evidence and the experience of Parties that have successfully implemented effective measures to reduce exposure to tobacco smoke.

The guidelines contain agreed upon statements of principles and definitions of relevant terms, as well as agreed upon recommendations for the steps required to satisfy the obligations of the Convention. In addition, the guidelines identify the measures necessary to achieve effective protection from the hazards of second-hand tobacco smoke. Parties are encouraged to use these guidelines not only to fulfil their legal duties under the Convention, but also to follow best practices in protecting public health.

Objectives of the guidelines

These guidelines have two related objectives. The first is to assist Parties in meeting their obligations under Article 8 of the WHO Framework Convention, in a manner consistent with the scientific evidence regarding exposure to second-hand tobacco smoke and the best practice worldwide in the implementation of smoke free measures, in order to establish a high standard of accountability for treaty compliance and to assist the Parties in promoting the highest attainable standard of health. The second objective is to identify the key elements of legislation necessary to effectively protect people from exposure to tobacco smoke, as required by Article 8.

Underlying considerations

The development of these guidelines has been influenced by the following fundamental considerations.

(a) The duty to protect from tobacco smoke, embodied in the text of Article 8, is grounded in fundamental human rights and freedoms. Given the dangers of breathing second-hand tobacco smoke, the duty to protect from tobacco smoke is implicit in, inter alia, the right to life and the

ARTICLE 8

right to the highest attainable standard of health, as recognized in many international legal instruments (including the Constitution of the World Health Organization, the Convention on the Rights of the Child, the Convention on the Elimination of all Forms of Discrimination against Women and the Covenant on Economic, Social and Cultural Rights), as formally incorporated into the preamble of the WHO Framework Convention and as recognized in the constitutions of many nations.

(b) The duty to protect individuals from tobacco smoke corresponds to an obligation by governments to enact legislation to protect individuals against threats to their fundamental rights and freedoms. This obligation extends to all persons, and not merely to certain populations.

(c) Several authoritative scientific bodies have determined that second-hand tobacco smoke is a carcinogen. Some Parties to the WHO Framework Convention (for example, Finland and Germany) have classified second-hand tobacco smoke as a carcinogen and included the prevention of exposure to it at work in their health and safety legislation. In addition to the requirements of Article 8, therefore, Parties may be obligated to address the hazard of exposure to tobacco smoke in accordance with their existing workplace laws or other laws governing exposure to harmful substances, including carcinogens.

STATEMENT OF PRINCIPLES AND RELEVANT DEFINITIONS UNDERLYING PROTECTION FROM EXPOSURE TO TOBACCO SMOKE

Principles

As noted in Article 4 of the WHO Framework Convention, strong political commitment is necessary to take measures to protect all persons from exposure to tobacco smoke. The following agreed upon principles should guide the implementation of Article 8 of the Convention.

Principle 1

Effective measures to provide protection from exposure to tobacco smoke, as envisioned by Article 8 of the WHO Framework Convention, require the total elimination of smoking and tobacco smoke in a particular space or environment in order to create a 100% smoke free environment. There is no safe level of exposure to tobacco smoke, and notions such as a threshold value for toxicity from second-hand smoke should be rejected, as they are contradicted by scientific evidence. Approaches other than 100% smoke free environments, including ventilation, air filtration and the use of designated smoking areas (whether with separate ventilation systems or not), have repeatedly been shown to be ineffective and there is conclusive evidence, scientific and otherwise, that engineering approaches do not protect against exposure to tobacco smoke.

Principle 2

All people should be protected from exposure to tobacco smoke. All indoor workplaces and indoor public places should be smoke free.

Principle 3

Legislation is necessary to protect people from exposure to tobacco smoke. Voluntary smoke free policies have repeatedly been shown to be ineffective and do not provide adequate protection. In order to be effective, legislation should be simple, clear and enforceable.

Principle 4

Good planning and adequate resources are essential for successful implementation and enforcement of smoke free legislation.

Principle 5

Civil society has a central role in building support for and ensuring compliance with smoke free measures, and should be included as an active partner in the process of developing, implementing and enforcing legislation.

Principle 6

The implementation of smoke free legislation, its enforcement and its impact should all be monitored and evaluated. This should include monitoring and responding to tobacco industry activities that undermine the implementation and enforcement of the legislation, as specified in Article 20.4 of the WHO Framework Convention.

Principle 7

The protection of people from exposure to tobacco smoke should be strengthened and expanded, if necessary; such action may include new or amended legislation, improved enforcement and other measures to reflect new scientific evidence and case-study experiences.

Definitions

In developing legislation, it is important to use care in defining key terms. Several recommendations as to appropriate definitions, based on experiences in many countries, are set out here. The definitions in this section supplement those already included in the WHO Framework Convention.

"Second-hand tobacco smoke" or "environmental tobacco smoke"

Several alternative terms are commonly used to describe the type of smoke addressed by Article 8 of the WHO Framework Convention. These include "second-hand smoke", "environmental tobacco smoke", and "other people's smoke". Terms such as "passive smoking" and "involuntary exposure to tobacco smoke" should be avoided, as experience in France and elsewhere suggests that the tobacco industry may use these terms to support a position that "voluntary" exposure is acceptable. "Second hand tobacco smoke", sometimes abbreviated as "SHS", and "environmental tobacco smoke", sometimes abbreviated "ETS", are the preferable terms; these guidelines use.

Second-hand tobacco smoke can be defined as "the smoke emitted from the burning end of a cigarette or from other tobacco products usually in combination with the smoke exhaled by the smoker".

"Smoke free air" is air that is 100% smoke free. This definition includes, but is not limited to, air in which tobacco smoke cannot be seen, smelled, sensed or measured.[1]

"Smoking"

This term should be defined to include being in possession or control of a lit tobacco product regardless of whether the smoke is being actively inhaled or exhaled.

"Public places"

While the precise definition of "public places" will vary between jurisdictions, it is important that legislation define this term as broadly as possible. The definition used should cover all places accessible to the general public or places for collective use, regardless of ownership or right to access.

"Indoor" or "enclosed"

Article 8 requires protection from tobacco smoke in "indoor" workplaces and public places. Because there are potential pitfalls in defining "indoor" areas, the experiences of various countries in defining this term should be specifically examined. The definition should be as inclusive and as clear as possible, and care should be taken in the definition to avoid creating lists that may be interpreted as excluding potentially relevant "indoor" areas. It is recommended that "indoor" (or "enclosed") areas be defined to include any space covered by a roof or enclosed by one or more walls or sides, regardless of the type of material used for the roof, wall or sides, and regardless of whether the structure is permanent or temporary.

"Workplace"

A "workplace" should be defined broadly as "any place used by people during their employment or work". This should include not only work done for compensation, but also voluntary work, if it is of the type for which compensation is normally paid. In addition, "workplaces" include not only

---

[1] It is possible that constituent elements of tobacco smoke may exist in air in amounts too small to be measured. Attention should be given to the possibility that the tobacco industry or the hospitality sector may attempt to exploit the limitations of this definition.

those places at which work is performed, but also all attached or associated places commonly used by the workers in the course of their employment, including, for example, corridors, lifts, stairwells, lobbies, joint facilities, cafeterias, toilets, lounges, lunchrooms and also outbuildings such as sheds and huts. Vehicles used in the course of work are workplaces and should be specifically identified as such.

Careful consideration should be given to workplaces that are also individuals' homes or dwelling places, for example, prisons, mental health institutions or nursing homes. These places also constitute workplaces for others, who should be protected from exposure to tobacco smoke.

"Public transport"

Public transport should be defined to include any vehicle used for the carriage of members of the public, usually for reward or commercial gain. This would include taxis.

THE SCOPE OF EFFECTIVE LEGISLATION

Principles

Article 8 requires the adoption of effective measures to protect people from exposure to tobacco smoke in (1) indoor workplaces, (2) indoor public places, (3) public transport, and (4) "as appropriate" in "other public places".

This creates an *obligation to provide universal protection* by ensuring that all indoor public places, all indoor workplaces, all public transport and possibly other (outdoor or quasi-outdoor) public places are free from exposure to second-hand tobacco smoke. No exemptions are justified on the basis of health or law arguments. If exemptions must be considered on the basis of other arguments, these should be minimal. In addition, if a Party is unable to achieve universal coverage immediately, Article 8 creates a continuing obligation to move as quickly as possible to remove any exemptions and make the protection universal. Each Party should strive to provide universal protection within five years of the WHO Framework Convention's entry into force for that Party.

No safe levels of exposure to second-hand smoke exist, and, as previously acknowledged by the Conference of the Parties in decision FCTC/COP1(15), engineering approaches, such as ventilation, air exchange and the use of designated smoking areas, do not protect against exposure to tobacco smoke.

Protection should be provided in all indoor or enclosed workplaces, including motor vehicles used as places of work (for example, taxis, ambulances or delivery vehicles).

The language of the treaty requires protective measures not only in all "indoor" public places, but also in those "other" (that is, outdoor or quasi-outdoor) public places where "appropriate". In identifying those outdoor and quasi-outdoor public places where legislation is appropriate, Parties should consider the evidence as to the possible health hazards in various settings and should act to adopt the most effective protection against exposure wherever the evidence shows that a hazard exists.

INFORM, CONSULT AND INVOLVE THE PUBLIC TO ENSURE SUPPORT AND SMOOTH IMPLEMENTATION

Raising awareness among the public and opinion leaders about the risks of second-hand tobacco smoke exposure through ongoing information campaigns is an important role for government agencies, in partnership with civil society, to ensure that the public understands and supports legislative action. Key stakeholders include businesses, restaurant and hospitality associations, employer groups, trade unions, the media, health professionals, organizations representing children and young people, institutions of learning or faith, the research community and the general public. Awareness-raising efforts should include consultation with affected businesses and other organizations and institutions in the course of developing the legislation.

Key messages should focus on the harm caused by second-hand tobacco smoke exposure, the fact that elimination of smoke indoors is the only science-based solution to ensure complete protection from exposure, the right of all workers to be equally protected by law and the fact that there is no trade-off between health and economics, because experience in an increasing number of jurisdictions shows that smoke free environments benefit both. Public education campaigns should also target settings for which legislation may not be feasible or appropriate, such as private homes.

Broad consultation with stakeholders is also essential to educate and mobilize the community and to facilitate support for legislation after its enactment. Once legislation is adopted, there should be an education campaign leading up to implementation of the law, the provision of information for business owners and building managers outlining the law and their responsibilities and the production of resources, such as signage. These measures will increase the likelihood of smooth implementation and high levels of voluntary compliance. Messages to empower non-smokers and to thank smokers for complying with the law will promote public involvement in enforcement and smooth implementation.

ENFORCEMENT

Duty of compliance

Effective legislation should impose legal responsibilities for compliance on both affected business establishments and individual smokers, and should provide penalties for violations, which should apply to businesses and, possibly, smokers. Enforcement should ordinarily focus on business establishments. The legislation should place the responsibility for compliance on the owner, manager or other person in charge of the premises, and should clearly identify the actions he or she is required to take. These duties should include:

(a) a duty to post clear signs at entrances and other appropriate locations indicating that smoking is not permitted. The format and content of these signs should be determined by health authorities or other agencies of the government and may identify a telephone number or other mechanisms for the public to report violations and the name of the person within the premises to whom complaints should be directed;

(b) a duty to remove any ashtrays from the premises;

(c) a duty to supervise the observance of rules;

(d) a duty to take reasonable specified steps to discourage individuals from smoking on the premises. These steps could include asking the person not to smoke, discontinuing service, asking the person to leave the premises and contacting a law enforcement agency or other authority.

Penalties

The legislation should specify fines or other monetary penalties for violations. While the size of these penalties will necessarily reflect the specific practices and customs of each country, several principles should guide the decision. Most importantly, penalties should be sufficiently large to deter violations or else they may be ignored by violators or treated as mere costs of doing business. Larger penalties are required to deter business violators than to deter violations by individual smokers, who usually have fewer resources. Penalties should increase for repeated violations and should be consistent with a country's treatment of other, equally serious offences.

In addition to monetary penalties, the legislation may also allow for administrative sanctions, such as the suspension of business licences, consistent with the country's practice and legal system. These "sanctions of last resort" are rarely used, but are very important for enforcing the law against any businesses that choose to defy the law repeatedly.

Criminal penalties for violations may be considered for inclusion, if appropriate within a country's legal and cultural context.

Enforcement infrastructure

Legislation should identify the authority or authorities responsible for enforcement, and should include a system both for monitoring compliance and for prosecuting violators.

Monitoring should include a process for inspection of businesses for compliance. It is seldom necessary to create a new inspection system for enforcement of smoke free legislation. Instead, compliance can ordinarily be monitored using one or more of the mechanisms already in place for inspecting business premises and workplaces. A variety of options usually exists for this purpose. In many countries, compliance inspections may be integrated into business licensing inspections, health and sanitation inspections, inspections for workplace health and safety, fire safety inspections or similar programmes. It may be valuable to use several such sources of information gathering simultaneously.

Where possible, the use of inspectors or enforcement agents at the local level is recommended; this is likely to increase the enforcement resources available and the level of compliance. This approach requires the establishment of a national coordinating mechanism to ensure a consistent approach nationwide.

Regardless of the mechanism used, monitoring should be based on an overall enforcement plan, and should include a process for effective training of inspectors. Effective monitoring may combine regular inspections with unscheduled, surprise inspections, as well as visits made in response to complaints. Such visits may well be educative in the early period after the law takes effect, as most breaches are likely to be inadvertent. The legislation should authorize inspectors to enter premises subject to the law and to collect samples and gather evidence, if these powers are not already established by existing law. Similarly, the legislation should prohibit businesses from obstructing the inspectors in their work.

The cost of effective monitoring is not excessive. It is not necessary to hire large numbers of inspectors, because inspections can be accomplished using existing programmes and personnel, and because experience shows that smoke free legislation quickly becomes self-enforcing (that is, predominantly enforced by the public). Only a few prosecutions may be necessary if the legislation is implemented carefully and active efforts are made to educate businesses and the public.

Although these programmes are not expensive, resources are needed to educate businesses, train inspectors, coordinate the inspection process and compensate personnel for inspections of businesses outside of normal working hours. A funding mechanism should be identified for this purpose. Effective monitoring programmes have used a variety of funding sources, including dedicated tax revenues, business licensing fees and dedicated revenues from fines paid by violators.

Enforcement strategies

Strategic approaches to enforcement can maximize compliance, simplify the implementation of legislation and reduce the level of enforcement resources needed.

In particular, enforcement activities in the period immediately following the law's entrance into force are critical to the law's success and to the success of future monitoring and enforcement. Many jurisdictions recommend an initial period of soft enforcement, during which violators are cautioned but not penalized. This approach should be combined with an active campaign to educate business owners about their responsibilities under the law, and businesses should understand that the initial grace period or phase-in period will be followed by more rigorous enforcement.

When active enforcement begins, many jurisdictions recommend the use of high-profile prosecutions to enhance deterrence. By identifying prominent violators who have actively defied the law or who are well known in the community, by taking firm and swift action and by seeking maximum public awareness of these activities, authorities are able to demonstrate their resolve and the seriousness of the law. This increases voluntary compliance and reduces the resources needed for future monitoring and enforcement.

While smoke free laws quickly become self-enforcing, it is nevertheless essential that authorities be prepared to respond swiftly and decisively to any isolated instances of outright defiance. Particularly when a law first comes into force, there may be an occasional violator who makes a public display of contempt for the law. Strong responses in these cases set an expectation of compliance that will ease future efforts, while indecisiveness can rapidly lead to widespread violations.

Mobilize and involve the community

The effectiveness of a monitoring-and-enforcement programme is enhanced by involving the community in the programme. Engaging the support of the community and encouraging members of the community to monitor compliance and report violations greatly extends the reach of enforcement agencies and reduces the resources needed to achieve compliance. In fact, in many jurisdictions, community complaints are the primary means of ensuring compliance. For this reason, smoke free legislation should specify that members of the public may initiate complaints and should authorize any person or nongovernmental organization to initiate action to compel compliance with measures regulating exposure to second-hand smoke. The enforcement programme should include a toll-free telephone complaint hotline or a similar system to encourage the public to report violations.

MONITORING AND EVALUATION OF MEASURES

Monitoring and evaluation of measures to reduce exposure to tobacco smoke are important for several reasons, for example:

(a) to increase political and public support for strengthening and extending legislative provisions;

(b) to document successes that will inform and assist the efforts of other countries;

(c) to identify and publicize the efforts made by the tobacco industry to undermine the implementation measures.

The extent and complexity of monitoring and evaluation will vary among jurisdictions, depending on available expertise and resources. However, it is important to evaluate the outcome of the measures implemented, in particular, on the key indicator of exposure to second-hand smoke in workplaces and public places. There may be cost-effective ways to achieve this, for example through the use of data or information collected through routine activities such as workplace inspections.

There are eight key process and outcome indicators that should be considered:[2]

Processes

(a) knowledge, attitudes and support for smoke free policies among the general population and possibly specific groups, for example, bar workers;

(b) enforcement of and compliance with smoke free policies;

Outcomes

(c) reduction in exposure of employees to second-hand tobacco smoke in workplaces and public places;

---

[2] The publication WHO policy recommendations: protection from exposure to second-hand tobacco smoke (Geneva, World Health Organization, 2007) provides references and links to monitoring studies conducted elsewhere on all of these indicators.

(d) reduction in content of second-hand tobacco smoke in the air in workplaces (particularly in restaurants) and public places;

(e) reduction in mortality and morbidity from exposure to second-hand tobacco smoke;

(f) reduction in exposure to second-hand tobacco smoke in private homes;

(g) changes in smoking prevalence and smoking-related behaviours;

(h) economic impacts.

LINKS TO SAMPLE LEGISLATION AND RESOURCE DOCUMENTS

References to the national and sub-national legislations currently in force that most closely conform to these best practice guidelines are provided below:

(a) United Kingdom of Great Britain and Northern Ireland, Health Act 2006, http://www.opsi.gov.uk/acts/acts2006/20060028.htm

(b) New Zealand, Smoke-free Environments Amendment Act 2003, http://www.legislation.govt.nz/browsc_vw.asp?content-set=pal_statutes

(c) Norway, Act No. 14 of 9 March 1973 relating to Prevention of the Harmful Effects of Tobacco,
http://odin.dep.no/hod/engelsk/regelverk/p20042245/042041-990030/dok-bn.html
(It should be noted, however, that the option of smoking sections is not recommended under these guidelines.)

(d) Scotland, Smoking, Health and Social Care (Scotland) Act 2005, http://www.opsi.gov.uk/legislation/scotland/acts2005/20050013.htm
Regulations: http://www.opsi.gov.uk/si/si2006/20061115.htm

(e) Uruguay, Decreto 40/006, http://www.globalsmokefreepartnership.org/files/132.doc

(f) Ireland, Public Health (Tobacco) (Amendment) Act 2004, http://193.178.1.79/2004/en/act/pub/0006/index.html

(g) Bermuda, Tobacco Products (Public Health) Amendment Act 2005, http://www.globalsmokefreepartnership.org/files/139.DOC

ARTICLE 8

Resource documents

1. WHO policy recommendations: protection from exposure to second-hand tobacco smoke. Geneva, World Health Organization, 2007.
http://www.who.int/tobacco/resources/publications/wntd/2007/who_ protection_exposure_ final_25June2007.pdf

2. Tobacco smoke and involuntary smoking. IARC Monographs on the Evolution of Carcinogenic Risks to Humans, Vol. 83, Lyon, France, World Health Organization and International Agency for Research on Cancer, 2004.
http://monographs.iarc.fr/ENG/Monographs/vol83/volume83.pdf

3. The health consequences of involuntary exposure to tobacco smoke: a report of the Surgeon General. Washington, DC, United States Department of Health and Human Services, 2006.
http://www.surgeongeneral.gov/library/secondhandsmoke/

4. Proposed identification of environmental tobacco smoke as a toxic air contaminant. San Francisco, United States of America, California Environmental Protection Agency: Air Resources Board, 2005.
http://repositories.cdlib.org/tc/surveys/CALEPA2005/

5. Joint briefing paper: Proposed guidelines for the implementation of Article 8 of the WHO Framework Convention on Tobacco Control. Framework Convention Alliance and the Global Smokefree Partnership, 2007.
http://www.fctc.org/x/documents/Article8_COP2_Briefing_English.pdf

6. Global Smokefree Partnership web site. A resource on smoke free success stories and challenges, this link includes perspectives on smoke free policies, links to evaluation reports, legislation and public information campaigns, as well as implementation guidelines.
www.globalsmokefreepartnership.org

7. After the smoke has cleared: evaluation of the impact of a new smoke free law. Wellington, New Zealand Ministry of Health, 2006.
http://www.moh.govt.nz/moh.nsf/by+unid/A9D3734516F6757ECC25723D0 0752D50?Open

Guidelines for implementation
Article 11

GUIDELINES FOR IMPLEMENTATION OF ARTICLE 11 OF THE WHO FRAMEWORK CONVENTION ON TOBACCO CONTROL

PACKAGING AND LABELLING OF TOBACCO PRODUCTS

PURPOSE, PRINCIPLES AND USE OF TERMS

Purpose

Consistent with other provisions of the WHO Framework Convention on Tobacco Control and the intentions of the Conference of the Parties to the Convention, these guidelines are intended to assist Parties in meeting their obligations under Article 11 of the Convention, and to propose measures that Parties can use to increase the effectiveness of their packaging and labelling measures. Article 11 stipulates that each Party shall adopt and implement effective packaging and labelling measures within a period of three years after entry into force of the Convention for that Party.

Principles

In order to achieve the objectives of the Convention and its protocols and to ensure successful implementation of its provisions, Article 4 of the Convention states that Parties shall be guided, inter alia, by the principle that every person should be informed of the health consequences, addictive nature and mortal threat posed by tobacco consumption and exposure to tobacco smoke.

Globally, many people are not fully aware of, misunderstand or underestimate the risks for morbidity and premature mortality due to tobacco use and exposure to tobacco smoke. Well-designed health warnings and messages on tobacco product packages have been shown to be a cost-effective means to increase public awareness of the health effects of tobacco use and to be effective in reducing tobacco consumption. Effective health warnings and messages and other tobacco product packaging and labelling measures are key components of a comprehensive, integrated approach to tobacco control.

Parties should consider the evidence and the experience of others when determining new packaging and labelling measures and aim to implement the most effective measures they can achieve.

As provided for in Articles 20 and 22 of the Convention, international collaboration and mutual support are fundamental principles for strengthening the capacity of Parties to implement fully and improve the effectiveness of Article 11 of the Convention.

Use of terms

For the purposes of these guidelines:

- "legal measures" means any legal instrument that contains or establishes obligations, requirements or prohibitions, according to the law of the relevant jurisdiction. Examples of such instruments include, but are not limited to acts, laws, regulations and administrative or executive orders;

- "insert" means any communication inside an individual package and/or carton purchased at retail by consumers, such as a miniature leaflet or brochure.

- "onsert" means any communication affixed to the outside of an individual package and/or carton purchased at retail by consumers, such as a miniature brochure beneath the outer cellophane wrapping or glued to the outside of the cigarette package.

DEVELOPING EFFECTIVE PACKAGING AND LABELLING REQUIREMENTS

Well-designed health warnings and messages are part of a range of effective measures to communicate health risks and to reduce tobacco use. Evidence demonstrates that the effectiveness of health warnings and messages increases with their prominence. In comparison with small, text-only health warnings, larger warnings with pictures are more likely to be noticed, better communicate health risks, provoke a greater emotional response and increase the motivation of tobacco users to quit and to decrease their tobacco consumption. Larger picture warnings are also more likely to retain their effectiveness over time and are particularly effective in communicating health effects to low-literacy populations, children and young people. Other elements that enhance effectiveness include locating health warnings and messages on principal display areas, and at the top of these principal display areas; the use of colour rather than just black and white; requiring that multiple health warnings and messages appear concurrently; and periodic revision of health warnings and messages.

Design elements

Location

Article 11.1(b)(iii) of the Convention specifies that each Party shall adopt and implement effective measures to ensure that health warnings and messages are large, clear, visible and legible. The location and layout of health warnings and messages on a package should ensure maximum visibility. Research indicates that health warnings and messages are more visible at the top rather than the bottom of the front and back of packages. Parties should require that health warnings and messages be positioned:

- on both the front and back (or on all main faces if there are more than two) of each unit packet and package, rather than just one side, to ensure that health warnings and messages are highly visible, recognizing that the frontal display area is the one most visible to the user for most package types;
- on principal display areas and, in particular, at the top of the principal display areas rather than at the bottom to increase visibility; and
- in such a way that normal opening of the package does not permanently damage or conceal the text or image of the health warning.

Parties should consider requiring, in addition to the health warnings and messages referred to in the previous paragraph, further health warnings and messages on all sides of a package, as well as on package inserts and onserts.

Parties should ensure that health warnings and messages are not obstructed by other required packaging and labelling markings or by commercial inserts and onserts. Parties should also ensure, when establishing the size and position of other markings, such as tax stamps and markings as per the requirements of Article 15 of the Convention, that such markings do not obstruct any part of the health warnings and messages.

Parties should consider introducing other innovative measures regarding location, including, but not limited to, requiring health warnings and messages to be printed on the filter overwrap portion of cigarettes and/or on other related materials such as packages of cigarette tubes, filters and papers as well as other instruments, such as those used for water pipe smoking.

Size

Article 11.1(b)(iv) of the Convention specifies that health warnings and messages on tobacco product packaging and labelling should be 50% or more, but no less than 30%, of the principal display areas. Given the evidence that the effectiveness of health warnings and messages increases with their size, Parties should consider using health warnings and messages that cover more than 50% of the principal display areas and aim to cover as much of the principal display areas as possible. The text of health warnings and messages should be in bold print in an easily legible font size and in a specified style and colour(s) that enhance overall visibility and legibility.

If a border is required, Parties should consider excluding the space dedicated to framing health warnings and messages from the size of the health warning or message itself when calculating the percentage of display area occupied by them, that is to say the space dedicated to the frame should be added to the total percentage of space occupied by the health warnings and messages and not included within it.

Use of pictorials

Article 11.1(b)(v) of the Convention specifies that health warnings and messages on tobacco product packaging and labelling may be in the form of or include pictures or pictograms. Evidence shows that health warnings and messages that contain both pictures and text are far more effective than those that are text-only. They also have the added benefit of potentially reaching people with low levels of literacy and those who cannot read the language(s) in which the text of the health warning or message is written. Parties should mandate culturally appropriate pictures or pictograms, in full colour, in their packaging and labelling requirements. Parties should consider the use of pictorial health warnings on both principal display areas (or on all main faces if there are more than two) of the tobacco products packaging.

Evidence shows that, when compared with text-only health warnings and messages, those with pictures:

- are more likely to be noticed;
- are rated more effective by tobacco users;
- are more likely to remain salient over time;
- better communicate the health risks of tobacco use;
- provoke more thought about the health risks of tobacco use and about cessation;
- increase motivation and intention to quit; and
- are associated with more attempts to quit.

Pictorial health warnings and messages may also disrupt the impact of brand imagery on packaging and decrease the overall attractiveness of the package.

When creating pictures for use on tobacco product packaging, Parties should obtain, where possible, ownership or full copyright of images, instead of allowing graphic designers or other sources to retain copyright. This provides maximum flexibility to use the images for other tobacco control interventions, including mass media campaigns and on the Internet. It may also enable Parties to grant licences to other jurisdictions to use the images.

Colour

The use of colour, as opposed to black and white, affects the overall noticeability of pictorial elements of health warnings and messages. Therefore, Parties should require full colour (four-colour printing), rather than black and white, for pictorial elements of health warnings and messages. Parties should select contrasting colours for the background of the text in order to enhance noticeability and maximize the legibility of text-based elements of health warnings and messages.

Rotation

Article 11.1(b)(ii) of the Convention specifies that health warnings and messages shall be rotating. Rotation can be implemented by having multiple health warnings and messages appearing concurrently or by setting a date after which the health warning and message content will change. Parties should consider using both types of rotation.

The novelty effect of new health warnings and messages is important, as evidence suggests that the impact of health warnings and messages that are repeated tends to decrease over time, whereas changes in health warnings and messages are associated with increased effectiveness. Rotation of health warnings and messages and changes in their layout and design are important to maintain saliency and enhance impact.

Parties should specify the number of health warnings and messages that are to appear concurrently. Parties should also require that health warnings and messages in a specified series be printed so that each appears on an equal number of retail packages, not just for each brand family but also for each brand within the brand family for each package size and type.

Parties should consider establishing two or more sets of health warnings and messages, specified from the outset, to alternate after a specified period, such as every 12–36 months. During transition periods, when an old set of health warnings and messages is being replaced by a new set, Parties should provide for a phase-in period for rotation between sets of health warnings and messages, during which time both sets may be used concurrently.

Message content

Using a range of health warnings and messages increases the likelihood of impact, as different health warnings and messages resonate with different people. Health warnings and messages should address different issues related to tobacco use, in addition to harmful health effects and the impact of exposure to tobacco smoke, such as:

- advice on cessation;
- the addictive nature of tobacco;
- adverse economic and social outcomes (for example, annual cost of purchasing tobacco products); and
- the impact of tobacco use on significant others (premature illness of one's father due to smoking, for example, or death of a loved one due to exposure to tobacco smoke).

Parties should also consider innovative content for other messages, such as adverse environmental outcomes and tobacco industry practices.

It is important to convey health warnings and messages in an effective manner; the tone should be authoritative and informative but non-judgemental. Health warnings and messages should also be presented in simple, clear and concise language that is culturally appropriate. Health warnings and messages can be presented in various formats, such as testimonials and positive and supportive information.

Evidence suggests that health warnings and messages are likely to be more effective if they elicit unfavourable emotional associations with tobacco use and when the information is personalized to make the health warnings and messages more believable and personally relevant. Health warnings and messages that generate negative emotions such as fear can be effective, particularly when combined with information designed to increase motivation and confidence in tobacco users in their ability to quit.

The provision of advice on cessation and specific sources for cessation help on tobacco packaging, such as a web site address or a toll-free telephone "quit line" number, can be important in helping tobacco users to change their behaviour.Parties should be aware that an increased demand for cessation-related services might require additional resources.

Language

Article 11.3 of the Convention specifies that each Party shall require that the warnings and other textual information specified in Article 11.1(b) and Article 11.2 appear on each unit packet and package of tobacco products, as well as on any outside packaging and labelling of such products, in the Party's principal language or languages.

In jurisdictions where there is more than one principal language, health warnings and messages can be displayed on each principal display area in more than one language, or, alternatively, a different language can be used for different principal display areas. Where appropriate, different languages or language combinations could also be used in different regions of a jurisdiction.

Source attribution

An attribution statement gives an identified source for the health warnings and messages on tobacco product packaging. There are, however, mixed views about whether they should form part of health warnings and messages. Some jurisdictions have provided a source attribution statement in order to increase the credibility of the health warnings and messages, while others have decided not to include a source attribution out of concern that it might detract from the impact of the warning. Where a source attribution statement is required, it is often located at the end of the health warning, in a smaller font size than the rest of the warning. Ultimately, Party-specific circumstances, such as beliefs and attitudes among target population subgroups, will determine whether the use of source attribution is likely to increase credibility or reduce impact.

If required, a source attribution statement should specify a credible expert source, such as the national health authority. The statement should be small enough not to detract from the overall noticeability and impact of the message, while being large enough to be legible.

Information on constituents and emissions

Article 11.2 of the Convention specifies that each unit packet and package of tobacco products, and any outside packaging and labelling of such products, shall, in addition to the warnings specified in Article 11.1(b), contain information on relevant constituents and emissions of tobacco products as defined by national authorities.

In implementing this obligation, Parties should require that relevant qualitative statements be displayed on each unit packet or package about the emissions of the tobacco product. Examples of such statements include "smoke from these cigarettes contains benzene, a known cancer-causing substance" and "smoking exposes you to more than 60 cancer-causing chemicals". Parties should also require that this information be shown on parts of the principal display areas or on an alternative display area (such as the side of packaging) not occupied by health warnings and messages.

Parties should not require quantitative or qualitative statements on tobacco product packaging and labelling about tobacco constituents and emissions that might imply that one brand is less harmful than another, such as the tar, nicotine and carbon monoxide figures or statements such as "these cigarettes contain reduced levels of nitrosamines".

The above three paragraphs should be read in conjunction with paragraphs below on "Preventing packaging and labelling that is misleading or deceptive".

PROCESS FOR DEVELOPING EFFECTIVE PACKAGING AND LABELLING REQUIREMENTS

Product category considerations

Article 11.1(b) of the Convention requires each Party to adopt and implement effective measures to ensure that each unit packet or package of tobacco products and any outside packaging and labelling of such products carry health warnings and messages. There should be no exemptions for small-volume companies or brands or for different types of tobacco products. Parties should consider requiring different health warnings and messages for different tobacco products such as cigarettes, cigars, smokeless tobacco, pipe tobacco, bidis and water pipe tobacco, in order to better focus on the specific health effects related to each product.

Different types of packaging

Parties should have a comprehensive understanding of the many different types of tobacco product packaging found within their jurisdiction, and should indicate how the proposed health warnings and messages will apply to each type and shape of packaging such as tins, boxes, pouches, flip-tops, slide and shell packages, cartons, transparent wrappers, clear packaging or packages containing one product unit.

Targeting population subgroups

Parties should consider designing warnings that target subgroups, such as youth, and adapting the number of health warnings and their rotation accordingly.

Pre-marketing testing

Depending on the available resources and time, Parties should consider pre-marketing testing to assess the effectiveness of the health warnings and messages on the intended target population. Pre-marketing testing can permit identification of unintended effects, such as inadvertently increasing the craving to smoke, and assessment of their cultural appropriateness. Consideration should be given to inviting civil society organizations not affiliated with the tobacco industry to contribute to this process. Ultimately, pre-marketing testing can be less costly than changes to legal measures at a later stage.

Parties should note that pre-marketing testing need not be long, complex or expensive. Valuable information can be obtained from simple focus groups of the target population, and Internet-based consultation is a quick and inexpensive alternative. Pre-marketing testing can be undertaken in parallel with the drafting of legal measures to avoid undue delay in implementation.

Public information and involvement

Parties should inform the public of proposals to introduce new health warnings and messages. Public support will assist Parties in introducing the new health warnings and messages. Parties should ensure, however, that public information and involvement do not unduly delay implementation of the Convention.

Supporting communication activity

The introduction of new health warnings and messages is more effective when it is coordinated with a broader, sustained public information and education campaign. Timely information should be provided to the media, as media coverage can increase the educational impact of new health warnings and messages.

DEVELOPING EFFECTIVE PACKAGING AND LABELLING RESTRICTIONS

Preventing packaging and labelling that is misleading or deceptive

Article 11.1(a) of the Convention specifies that Parties shall adopt and implement, in accordance with their national law, effective measures to ensure that tobacco product packaging and labelling do not promote a tobacco product by any means that are false, misleading, deceptive or likely to create an erroneous impression about the product's characteristics, health effects, hazards or emissions, including any term, descriptor, trademark or figurative or other sign that directly or indirectly creates the false impression that a particular tobacco product is less harmful than others. These may include terms such as "low tar", "light", "ultra-light" or "mild", this list being indicative but not exhaustive. In implementing the obligations pursuant to Article 11.1(a), Parties are not limited to prohibiting the terms specified but should also prohibit terms such as "extra", "ultra" and similar terms in any language that might mislead consumers.

Parties should prohibit the display of figures for emission yields (such as tar, nicotine and carbon monoxide) on packaging and labelling, including when used as part of a brand name or trademark. Tar, nicotine and other smoke emission yields derived from smoking-machine testing do not provide valid estimates of human exposure. In addition, there is no conclusive epidemiological or scientific evidence that cigarettes with lower machine-generated smoke yields are less harmful than cigarettes with higher smoke emission yields. The marketing of cigarettes with stated tar and nicotine yields has resulted in the mistaken belief that those cigarettes are less harmful.

Parties should prevent the display of expiry dates on tobacco packaging and labelling where this misleads or deceives consumers into concluding that tobacco products are safe to be consumed at any time.

Plain packaging

Parties should consider adopting measures to restrict or prohibit the use of logos, colours, brand images or promotional information on packaging other than brand names and product names displayed in a standard colour and font style (plain packaging). This may increase the noticeability and effectiveness of health warnings and messages, prevent the package from detracting attention from them, and address industry package design techniques that may suggest that some products are less harmful than others.

LEGAL MEASURES

Drafting

In drafting legal measures with respect to tobacco product packaging and labelling, Parties should consider issues such as who will be responsible for their administration, the available approaches for ensuring compliance and enforcement, and the level or levels of government involved.

Administration

Parties should identify the authority or authorities responsible for overseeing implementation of tobacco product packaging and labelling measures. Parties should consider ensuring that the relevant authority responsible for tobacco control matters is the same as that which administers the legal measures. In the event that the administration is made the responsibility of another area of government, the relevant health authority should provide input into label specifications.

Scope

Parties should ensure that the packaging and labelling provisions related to Article 11 of the Convention apply equally to all tobacco products sold within the jurisdiction, and that no distinction is made between products that are manufactured domestically or imported or intended for duty-free sale within a Party's jurisdiction. Parties should consider circumstances in which measures would apply to exported products.

Costs

Parties should ensure that the cost of placing health warnings and messages, as well as information on constituents and emissions, on tobacco product packaging is borne by the tobacco industry.

Liability

Consistent with Article 19 of the Convention, Parties should consider including provisions to make it clear that the requirement to carry health warnings and messages or to convey any other information about a tobacco product does not remove or diminish any obligation of the tobacco industry, including, but not limited to, obligations to warn consumers about the health hazards arising from tobacco use and exposure to tobacco smoke.

Specific provisions

Parties should ensure that clear, detailed specifications are provided for in their legal measures in order to limit the opportunity for tobacco manufacturers and importers to deviate in the implementation of health warnings and messages, as well as to prevent inconsistencies among tobacco products. In drafting such measures, Parties should review, inter alia, the following list:

- packaging and products (please refer to paragraph above on "Different types of packaging";
- language(s) to be used in mandated text of health warnings and messages and in information on constituents and emissions on packaging, including how languages should appear if there is more than one language;
- rotation practice and time frames, including the number of health warnings and messages to appear concurrently as well as specifications of transition periods and deadlines within which the new health warnings and messages must appear;
- distribution practices, in order to obtain equal display of health warnings and messages on retail packages, not just for each brand family but also for each brand within the brand family for each package size and type;
- how text, pictures and pictograms of health warnings and messages should actually appear on packaging (including specification of location, wording, size, colour, font, layout, print quality), including package inserts, onserts and interior messages;
- different health warnings and messages for different types of tobacco product, where appropriate;
- source attribution, if appropriate, including placement, text and font (similar detailed specifications as for the health warnings and messages themselves); and
- prohibition of promotion by means that are false, misleading, deceptive or likely to create an erroneous impression, in accordance with Article 11.1(a) of the Convention.

Source document

Parties should consider providing a "source document", which contains high-quality visual samples of how all health warnings and messages and other information are to appear on packaging. A source document is particularly useful in the event that the language used in the legal measures is not sufficiently clear.

Adhesive labels and covers

Parties should ensure that adhesive labels, stickers, cases, covers, sleeves, wrapping and tobacco manufacturers' promotional inserts and onserts do not obscure, obliterate or undermine health warnings and messages. For example, adhesive labels might be allowed only if they cannot be removed and are used only on metal or wood containers that hold products other than cigarettes.

Legal responsibility for compliance

Parties should specify that tobacco product manufacturers, importers, wholesalers and retail establishments that sell tobacco products bear legal responsibility for compliance with packaging and labelling measures.

Penalties

In order to deter non-compliance with the law, Parties should specify a range of fines or other penalties commensurate with the severity of the violation and whether it is a repeat violation.
Parties should consider introducing any other penalty consistent with a Party's legal system and culture that may include the creation and enforcement of offences and the suspension, limitation or cancellation of business and import licences.

Enforcement powers

Parties should consider granting enforcement authorities the power to order violators to recall non-compliant tobacco products, and to recover all expenses stemming from the recall, as well as the power to impose whatever sanctions are deemed appropriate, including seizure and destruction of non-compliant products. Further, Parties should consider making public the names of violators and the nature of their offence.

Supply deadline

In order to ensure the timely introduction of health warnings and messages, legal measures should specify a single deadline by which manufacturers, importers, wholesalers and retailers must only supply tobacco products that comply with the new requirements. The time allocated need only be enough to allow manufacturers and importers to organize the printing of new packages. It has been considered that a period of up to 12 months from the enactment of the legal measures should suffice in most circumstances.

Review

Parties should recognize that the drafting of legal measures for packaging and labelling of tobacco products is not a one-time exercise. Legal measures should be reviewed periodically and updated as new evidence emerges and as specific health warnings and messages wear out. When undertaking periodic reviews or updates, Parties should take into account their experience in using their packaging and labelling measures, the experiences of other jurisdictions, as well as industry practices in this area. Such reviews or updates can help identify weaknesses and loopholes and highlight areas in which the language used in the measures should be clarified.

ENFORCEMENT

Infrastructure and budget

Parties should consider ensuring that the infrastructure necessary for compliance and enforcement activities exists. Parties should also consider providing a budget for such activities.

Strategies

To enhance compliance, Parties should inform stakeholders of the requirements of the law before it comes into force. Different strategies might be required for different stakeholders, such as tobacco manufacturers, importers and retailers.

Parties should consider using inspectors or enforcement agents to conduct regular spot checks of tobacco products at manufacturing and importing facilities, as well as at points of sale, to ensure that packaging and labelling comply with the law. It may not be necessary to create a new inspection system if mechanisms are already in place that could be extended to inspect business premises as required. Where applicable, stakeholders should be informed that tobacco products will undergo regular spot checks at points of sale.

Response to non-compliance

Parties should ensure that their enforcement authorities are prepared to respond quickly and decisively to instances of non-compliance. Strong, timely responses to early cases will make it clear that compliance is expected and will facilitate future enforcement. Parties should consider making the results of enforcement action public in order to send a strong message that non-compliance will be investigated and action will be taken.

Complaints

Parties should consider encouraging the public to report violations in order to further promote compliance with the law. It might be helpful to establish an enforcement contact point for reporting alleged cases of non-compliance. Parties should ensure that complaints are investigated and dealt with in a timely and thorough manner.

MONITORING AND EVALUATING PACKAGING AND LABELLING MEASURES

Parties should consider monitoring and evaluating their packaging and labelling measures to assess their impact as well as to identify where improvements are needed. Monitoring and evaluation also contribute to the body of evidence that can assist the efforts of other Parties in implementing their packaging and labelling measures.

Monitoring of the tobacco industry's compliance should be initiated immediately after legal measures have come into force and should be conducted continuously thereafter.

Impact on populations

It is important to assess the impact of packaging and labelling measures on the target populations. Parties should consider measuring aspects such as noticeability, comprehension, credibility, informativeness, recall and personal relevance of health warnings and messages, health knowledge and perceptions of risks, intentions to change behaviour and actual behavioural changes.

Baseline and follow-up

Parties should consider adopting strategies to evaluate the impact of packaging and labelling measures both before and at regular intervals after they are implemented.

Resources

The extent and complexity of actions to evaluate the impact of tobacco product packaging and labelling measures will vary among Parties, depending on the objectives and the availability of resources and expertise.

Dissemination

Parties should consider publishing, or making available to other Parties and to the public, the results gathered from monitoring of compliance and evaluating impact.

INTERNATIONAL COOPERATION

International cooperation is essential for progress in such an important, constantly changing area as tobacco control. Several articles of the Convention provide for exchanges of knowledge and experience to promote progress in implementation, with a particular focus on the needs of developing country Parties and Parties with economies in transition. Cooperation among Parties to promote the transfer of technical, scientific and legal expertise and technology, as required by Article 22, would strengthen the implementation of Article 11 of the Convention globally. One example of such cooperation would be the provision of licences quickly, easily and without cost from Parties to other jurisdictions seeking to use their pictorial health warnings. International cooperation would also help to ensure that consistent and accurate information relating to tobacco products is provided globally.

Parties should endeavour to share legal and other expertise in countering tobacco industry arguments against packaging and labelling measures.

Parties should consider reviewing the reports of other Parties, pursuant to Article 21 of the Convention, to enhance their knowledge of international experience with respect to packaging and labelling.

Guidelines for implementation
Article 13

GUIDELINES FOR IMPLEMENTATION OF ARTICLE 13 OF THE WHO FRAMEWORK CONVENTION ON TOBACCO CONTROL

TOBACCO ADVERTISING, PROMOTION AND SPONSORSHIP

PURPOSE AND OBJECTIVES

The purpose of these guidelines is to assist Parties in meeting their obligations under Article 13 of the WHO Framework Convention on Tobacco Control. They draw on the best available evidence and the experience of Parties that have successfully implemented effective measures against tobacco advertising, promotion and sponsorship. They give Parties guidance for introducing and enforcing a comprehensive ban on tobacco advertising, promotion and sponsorship or, for those Parties that are not in a position to undertake a comprehensive ban owing to their constitutions or constitutional principles, for applying restrictions on tobacco advertising, promotion and sponsorship that are as comprehensive as possible.

These guidelines provide guidance on the best ways to implement Article 13 of the Convention in order to eliminate tobacco advertising, promotion and sponsorship effectively at both domestic and international levels.

The following principles apply:

(a) It is well documented that tobacco advertising, promotion and sponsorship increase tobacco use and that comprehensive bans on tobacco advertising, promotion and sponsorship decrease tobacco use.

(b) An effective ban on tobacco advertising, promotion and sponsorship should, as recognized by Parties to the Convention in Articles 13.1 and 13.2, be *comprehensive* and applicable to *all* tobacco advertising, promotion and sponsorship.

(c) According to the definitions in Article 1 of the Convention, a comprehensive ban on all tobacco advertising, promotion and sponsorship applies to *all* forms of *commercial communication, recommendation or action* and all forms of *contribution* to any event, activity or individual with the *aim, effect, or likely effect* of promoting a tobacco product or tobacco use either *directly or indirectly.*

(d) A comprehensive ban on tobacco advertising, promotion and sponsorship should include *cross-border advertising, promotion and sponsorship.* This includes both out-flowing advertising, promotion and sponsorship (originating from a Party's territory) and in-flowing advertising, promotion and sponsorship (entering a Party's territory).

(e) To be effective, a comprehensive ban should address *all persons or entities* involved in the production, placement and/or dissemination of tobacco advertising, promotion and sponsorship.

(f) Effective *monitoring, enforcement and sanctions* supported and facilitated by strong *public education and community awareness programmes* are essential for implementation of a comprehensive ban on tobacco advertising, promotion and sponsorship.

(g) *Civil society* has a central role in building support for, developing and ensuring compliance with laws addressing tobacco advertising, promotion and sponsorship, and it should be included as an active partner in this process.

(h) Effective *international cooperation* is fundamental to the elimination of both domestic and cross-border tobacco advertising, promotion and sponsorship.

SCOPE OF A COMPREHENSIVE BAN

The scope of a comprehensive ban on tobacco advertising, promotion and sponsorship is outlined in general terms in subsection "Overview" below, while the subsections from "Retail sale and display" to "Communication within the tobacco trade" inclusive address aspects that could pose special challenges for regulators in introducing a comprehensive ban.

Overview

A ban on tobacco advertising, promotion and sponsorship is effective only if it has a broad scope. Contemporary marketing communication involves an integrated approach to advertising and promoting the purchase and sale of goods, including direct marketing, public relations, sales promotion, personal selling and online interactive marketing methods. If only certain forms of direct tobacco advertising are prohibited, the tobacco industry inevitably shifts its expenditure to other advertising, promotion and sponsorship strategies, using creative, indirect ways to promote tobacco products and tobacco use, especially among young people.

Therefore, the effect of a partial advertising ban on tobacco consumption is limited. This is recognized in Article 13 of the Convention, which lays down the basic obligation to ban tobacco advertising, promotion and sponsorship. According to Article 13.1 of the Convention, "Parties recognize that a comprehensive ban on advertising, promotion and sponsorship would reduce the consumption of tobacco products".

To implement the comprehensive ban laid down in Articles 13.1 and 13.2 of the Convention, Parties should ban advertising, promotion and sponsorship as defined in Article 1(c) and (g) of the Convention. Article 1(c) defines "tobacco advertising and promotion" as "any form of commercial communication, recommendation or action with the aim, effect or likely effect of promoting a tobacco product or tobacco use either directly or indirectly". Article 1(g) defines "tobacco sponsorship" as "any form of contribution to any event, activity or individual with the aim, effect or likely effect of promoting a tobacco product or tobacco use either directly or indirectly".

It is important to note that both "tobacco advertising and promotion" and "tobacco sponsorship" cover promotion not only of particular tobacco products but also of tobacco use generally; not only acts with a promotional aim but also acts that have a promotional effect or are likely to have a promotional effect; and not only direct promotion but also indirect promotion. "Tobacco advertising and promotion" is not restricted to "communications", but also includes "recommendations" and "actions", which should cover at least the following categories: (a) various sales and/or distribution arrangements[9]; (b) hidden forms of advertising or promotion, such as insertion of tobacco products or tobacco use in various media contents; (c) association of tobacco products with events or with other products in various ways; (d) promotional packaging and product design features; and (e) production and distribution of items such as sweets and toys or other products that resemble cigarettes or other tobacco products.[1] It is also important to note that the definition of "tobacco sponsorship" covers "any form of contribution", financial or otherwise, regardless of how or whether that contribution is acknowledged or publicized.

Promotional effects, both direct and indirect, may be brought about by the use of words, designs, images, sounds and colours, including brand names, trademarks, logos, names of tobacco manufacturers or importers, and colours or schemes of colours associated with tobacco products, manufacturers or importers, or by the use of a part or parts of words, designs, images and colours. Promotion of tobacco companies themselves (sometimes referred to as corporate promotion) is a form of promotion of tobacco products or tobacco use, even without the presentation of brand names or trademarks. Advertising, including display and sponsorship of smoking accessories such as cigarette papers, filters and equipment for rolling cigarettes, as well as imitations of tobacco products, may also have the effect of promoting tobacco products or tobacco use.

Legislation should avoid providing lists of prohibited activities that are, or could be understood to be, exhaustive. While it is often useful to provide examples of prohibited activities, when legislation does so, it should make clear that they are only examples and do not cover the full range of prohibited activities. This can be made clear by using terms like "including but not limited to" or catch-all phrases such as "or any other form of tobacco advertising, promotion or sponsorship".

---

[1] For instance, incentive schemes for retailers, display at points of sale, lotteries, free gifts, free samples, discounts, competitions (whether the purchase of tobacco products is required or not) and incentive promotions or loyalty schemes, e.g. redeemable coupons provided with purchase of tobacco products.

An indicative (non-exhaustive) list of forms of advertising, promotion and sponsorship that fall under the ban in Article 13 of the Convention is attached in the appendix to these guidelines.

Recommendation

A comprehensive ban on tobacco advertising, promotion and sponsorship, should cover:

- all advertising and promotion, as well as sponsorship, without exemption;
- direct and indirect advertising, promotion and sponsorship;
- acts that aim at promotion and acts that have or are likely to have a promotional effect;
- promotion of tobacco products and the use of tobacco;
- commercial communications and commercial recommendations and actions;
- contribution of any kind to any event, activity or individual;
- advertising and promotion of tobacco brand names and all corporate promotion; and
- traditional media (print, television and radio) and all media platforms, including Internet, mobile telephones and other new technologies as well as films.

Retail sale and display

Display of tobacco products at points of sale in itself constitutes advertising and promotion. Display of products is a key means of promoting tobacco products and tobacco use, including by stimulating impulse purchases of tobacco products, giving the impression that tobacco use is socially acceptable and making it harder for tobacco users to quit. Young people are particularly vulnerable to the promotional effects of product display.

To ensure that points of sale of tobacco products do not have any promotional elements, Parties should introduce a total ban on any display and on the visibility of tobacco products at points of sale, including fixed retail outlets and street vendors. Only the textual listing of products and their prices, without any promotional elements, would be allowed. As for all aspects of Article 13 of the Convention, the ban should also apply in ferries, airplanes, ports and airports.

---

[2] This text reflects the spirit of Article 16.1 of the Convention, which obliges Parties to "adopt and implement effective legislative, executive, administrative or other measures at the appropriate government level to prohibit sales of tobacco products to persons under the age set by domestic law, national law or eighteen. These measures may include [...] (c) prohibiting the manufacture and sale of sweets, snacks, toys or any other object in the form of tobacco products which appeal to minors".

Vending machines should be banned because they constitute by their very presence a means of advertising or promotion under the terms of the Convention.[3]

Recommendation

Display and visibility of tobacco products at points of sale constitutes advertising and promotion and should therefore be banned. Vending machines should be banned because they constitute, by their very presence, a means of advertising and promotion.

Packaging and product features[4]

Packaging is an important element of advertising and promotion. Tobacco pack or product features are used in various ways to attract consumers, to promote products and to cultivate and promote brand identity, for example by using logos, colours, fonts, pictures, shapes and materials on or in packs or on individual cigarettes or other tobacco products.

The effect of advertising or promotion on packaging can be eliminated by requiring plain packaging: black and white or two other contrasting colours, as prescribed by national authorities; nothing other than a brand name, a product name and/or manufacturer's name, contact details and the quantity of product in the packaging, without any logos or other features apart from health warnings, tax stamps and other government-mandated information or markings; prescribed font style and size; and standardized shape, size and materials. There should be no advertising or promotion inside or attached to the package or on individual cigarettes or other tobacco products.

If plain packaging is not yet mandated, the restriction should cover as many as possible of the design features that make tobacco products more attractive to consumers such as animal or other figures, "fun" phrases, coloured cigarette papers, attractive smells, novelty or seasonal packs.

Recommendation

Packaging and product design are important elements of advertising and promotion. Parties should consider adopting plain packaging requirements to eliminate the effects of advertising or promotion on packaging. Packaging, individual cigarettes or other tobacco products should carry no advertising or promotion, including design features that make products attractive.

---

[3] Banning vending machines because they amount to advertising or promotion complements the provisions of Article 16 of the Convention on protecting minors. The possible measures described in Article 16.1 include "ensuring that tobacco vending machines under [each Party's] jurisdiction are not accessible to minors and do not promote sale of tobacco products to minors"; and Article 16.5 stipulates that "… a Party may, by means of a binding written declaration, indicate its commitment to prohibit the introduction of tobacco vending machines within its jurisdiction or, as appropriate, to a total ban on tobacco vending machines".

[4] See also the guidelines for implementation of Article 11 of the Convention, which address plain packaging with regard to health warnings and misleading information.

Internet sales

Internet sales of tobacco inherently involve advertising and promotion as defined in the Convention. The problem is not only limited to advertising and promotion but also includes sales to minors, tax evasion and illicit trade.

The most direct way of avoiding tobacco advertising or promotion on the Internet is to ban tobacco sales on the Internet.[5] The ban should apply not only to entities that sell the products but also to others, including credit card companies that facilitate payment and postal or delivery services for the products.

To the extent that Internet sales are not yet banned, restrictions should be imposed, allowing only textual listing of products with prices, with no pictures or promotion features (e.g. any references to low prices).

Given the covert nature of tobacco advertising and promotion on the Internet and the difficulty of identifying and reaching wrongdoers, special domestic resources are needed to make these measures operational. Measures recommended in decision FCTC/COP3(14) to eliminate cross-border tobacco advertising, promotion and sponsorship, in particular identifying contact points and dealing with notifications from other Parties, would help to ensure that domestic enforcement efforts are not undermined.

> *Recommendation*
> Internet sales of tobacco should be banned as they inherently involve tobacco advertising and promotion.

Brand stretching and brand sharing

"Brand stretching" occurs when a tobacco brand name, emblem, trademark, logo or trade insignia or any other distinctive feature (including distinctive colour combinations) is connected with a non-tobacco product or service in such a way that the tobacco product and the non-tobacco product or service are likely to be associated.

"Brand sharing" occurs when a brand name, emblem, trademark, logo or trade insignia or any other distinctive feature (including distinctive colour combinations) on a non-tobacco product or service is connected with a tobacco product or tobacco company in such a way that the tobacco product or company and the non-tobacco product or service are likely to be associated.

"Brand stretching" and "brand sharing" should be regarded as tobacco advertising and promotion in so far as they have the aim, effect or likely effect of promoting a tobacco product or tobacco use either directly or indirectly.

---

[5] Options for regulating Internet sales are being discussed by the Intergovernmental Negotiating Body on a Protocol on Illicit Trade in Tobacco Products.

Recommendation

Parties should ban "brand stretching" and "brand sharing", as they are means of tobacco advertising and promotion.

Corporate social responsibility[6]

It is increasingly common for tobacco companies to seek to portray themselves as good corporate citizens by making contributions to deserving causes or by otherwise promoting "socially responsible" elements of their business practices.

Some tobacco companies make financial or in-kind contributions to organizations, such as community, health, welfare or environmental organizations, either directly or through other entities. Such contributions fall within the definition of tobacco sponsorship in Article 1(g) of the Convention and should be prohibited as part of a comprehensive ban, because the aim, effect or likely effect of such a contribution is to promote a tobacco product or tobacco use either directly or indirectly.

Tobacco companies may also seek to engage in "socially responsible" business practices (such as good employee–employer relations or environmental stewardship), which do not involve contributions to other parties. Promotion to the public of such otherwise commendable activities should be prohibited, as their aim, effect or likely effect is to promote a tobacco product or tobacco use either directly or indirectly. Public dissemination of such information should be prohibited, except for the purposes of required corporate reporting (such as annual reports) or necessary business administration (e.g. for recruitment purposes and communications with suppliers).

Tobacco industry public education campaigns, such as "youth smoking prevention campaigns" should be prohibited on the basis that they involve "contributions" when implemented by other parties or represent corporate promotion if conducted by the industry itself.

Recommendation

The Parties should ban contributions from tobacco companies to any other entity for "socially responsible causes", as this is a form of sponsorship. Publicity given to "socially responsible" business practices of the tobacco industry should be banned, as it constitutes advertising and promotion.

---

[6] The guidelines on Article 5.3 of the Convention, elaborated by a working group established by the Conference of the Parties, address this subject from the perspective of protecting public health policies with respect to tobacco control from commercial and other vested interests of the tobacco industry

Legitimate expression

Implementation of a comprehensive ban on tobacco advertising, promotion and sponsorship should not prevent legitimate journalistic, artistic or academic expression or legitimate social or political commentary. Examples include news images with coincidental tobacco-related content in the background, the depiction of historical personalities or presentation of views on regulation or policy. Nevertheless, appropriate warnings or disclaimers may be required. In some cases, journalistic, artistic or academic expression or social or political commentary may contain elements that are not justified for editorial, artistic, academic, social or political reasons and must be regarded as advertising, promotion or sponsorship rather than genuine editorial, artistic or academic content or genuine social or political commentary. This is obviously the case if an insertion is made for commercial, tobacco-related reasons, for example, paid placement of tobacco products or images in the media.

Recommendation

Implementation of a comprehensive ban on tobacco advertising, promotion and sponsorship need not interfere with legitimate types of expression, such as journalistic, artistic or academic expression or legitimate social or political commentary. Parties should, however, take measures to prevent the use of journalistic, artistic or academic expression or social or political commentary for the promotion of tobacco use or tobacco products.

Depictions of tobacco in entertainment media

The depiction of tobacco in entertainment media products, such as films, theatre and games, can strongly influence tobacco use, particularly among young people. Therefore, Parties should take the following measures:

- Implement a mechanism requiring that when an entertainment media product depicts tobacco products, use or imagery of any type, the responsible executives at each company involved in the production, distribution or presentation of that entertainment media product certify that no money, gifts, free publicity, interest-free loans, tobacco products, public relations assistance or anything else of any value has been given in exchange for the depiction.

- Prohibit the depiction of identifiable tobacco brands or tobacco brand images in association with, or as part of the content of, any entertainment media product.

- Require the display of prescribed anti-tobacco advertisements at the beginning of any entertainment media product that depicts tobacco products, use or images.

- Implement a ratings or classification system that takes into account the depiction of tobacco products, use or images in rating or classifying entertainment media products (for example, requiring adult ratings which restrict access of minors) and that ensures that entertainment media aimed at children (including cartoons) do not depict tobacco products, use or imagery.

Recommendation

Parties should take particular measures concerning the depiction of tobacco in entertainment media products, including requiring certification that no benefits have been received for any tobacco depictions, prohibiting the use of identifiable tobacco brands or imagery, requiring anti-tobacco advertisements and implementing a ratings or classification system that takes tobacco depictions into account.

Communication within the tobacco trade

The objective of banning tobacco advertising, promotion and sponsorship can usually be achieved without banning communications within the tobacco trade.

Any exception to a comprehensive ban on tobacco advertising, promotion and sponsorship for the purpose of providing product information to actors within the tobacco trade should be defined and applied strictly. Access to such information should be restricted to those persons who make trading decisions and who consequently need the information.

Tobacco manufacturers' newsletters can be exempted from the comprehensive ban on tobacco advertising, promotion and sponsorship, but only if they are destined exclusively for the manufacturer's employees, contractors, suppliers and other business partners and only to the extent that their distribution is limited to those persons or entities.

Recommendation

Any exception to a comprehensive ban on tobacco advertising, promotion and sponsorship to allow communication within the tobacco trade should be defined and applied strictly.

Constitutional principles in relation to a comprehensive ban

Any Party whose constitution or constitutional principles impose constraints on undertaking a comprehensive ban should, under Article 13 of the Convention, apply restrictions that are as comprehensive as possible in the light of those constraints. All Parties are obliged to undertake a comprehensive ban unless they are "not in a position" to do so *due to* [their] constitution or constitutional principles". This obligation is to be interpreted in the context of the "recogni[tion] that a comprehensive ban on advertising, promotion and sponsorship would reduce the consumption of tobacco products", and in the light of the Convention's overall objective "to protect present and future generations from the devastating health, social, environmental and economic consequences of tobacco consumption and exposure to tobacco smoke" (Article 3 of the Convention).

It is acknowledged that the question of how constitutional principles are to be accommodated is to be determined by each Party's constitutional system.

OBLIGATIONS RELATED TO ARTICLE 13.4 OF THE CONVENTION

Under Articles 13.2 and 13.3 of the Convention, Parties are obliged to undertake a comprehensive ban on tobacco advertising, promotion and sponsorship (or apply restrictions that are as comprehensive as possible in light of their constitution or constitutional principles). Some forms of tobacco advertising, promotion and sponsorship can be expected to persist in Parties that have not yet met their obligations under Articles 13.2 and 13.3 of the Convention. In addition, some very limited forms of relevant commercial communication, recommendation or action might continue to exist after a comprehensive ban has been implemented, and some forms of tobacco advertising, promotion and sponsorship may continue in Parties whose constitutions or constitutional principles prevent a comprehensive ban.

Any form of tobacco advertising, promotion or sponsorship that is not prohibited is obliged to meet the requirements of Article 13.4 of the Convention. Notably, these requirements include to "prohibit all forms of tobacco advertising, promotion and sponsorship that promote a tobacco product by any means that are false, misleading or deceptive or likely to create an erroneous impression about its characteristics, health effects, hazards or emissions" (13.4(a)); to "require that health or other appropriate warnings or messages accompany all tobacco advertising and, as appropriate, promotion and sponsorship" (13.4(b)); and to "require, if [a Party] does not have a comprehensive ban, the disclosure to relevant governmental authorities of expenditures by the tobacco industry on advertising, promotion and sponsorship not yet prohibited" (13.4(d)).

Parties should prohibit the use of any term, descriptor, trademark, emblem, marketing image, logo, colour and figurative or any other sign[7] that promotes a tobacco product or tobacco use, whether directly or indirectly, by any means that are false, misleading or deceptive or likely to create an erroneous impression about the characteristics, health effects, hazards or emissions of any tobacco product or tobacco products, or about the health effects or hazards of tobacco use. Such a prohibition should cover, inter alia, use of the terms "low tar", "light", "ultra-light", "mild", "extra", "ultra" and other terms in any language that may be misleading or create an erroneous impression.[8]

Parties should consider giving health or other warnings and messages accompanying any tobacco advertising, promotion and sponsorship at least equal prominence to the advertising, promotion or sponsorship. The content of the required warnings and messages should be prescribed by the relevant authorities and should effectively communicate the health risks and addictiveness of tobacco use, discourage the use of tobacco products and increase motivation to quit tobacco use. In order to maximize their effectiveness, the warnings or other messages required by Parties under

---

[7] These phrases are taken from Article 11.1(a) of the Convention, with the addition of the word "colour", which the working group recognizes can be used to convey a misleading impression about the characteristics, health effects or hazards of tobacco products.

[8] See Article 11.1(a) and the guidelines on Article 11 of the Convention.

Article 13.4(b) of the Convention should be consistent with the warnings or other messages on packaging that the Convention requires under Article 11.

Parties should require disclosure by the tobacco industry to relevant governmental authorities of any advertising, promotion and sponsorship in which it engages. The disclosures should be made at regular intervals prescribed by law and in response to specific requests. They should include, both in total and by brand, information about:

- the kind of advertising, promotion or sponsorship, including its content, form and type of media;
- the placement and extent or frequency of the advertising, promotion or sponsorship;
- the identity of all entities involved in the advertising, promotion and sponsorship, including advertising and production companies;
- in the case of cross-border advertising, promotion or sponsorship originating from a Party's territory, the territory or territories in which it is intended to be, or may be, received; and
- the amount of financial or other resources used for the advertising, promotion or sponsorship.

Parties should make the information readily available to the public (e.g. via the Internet)[9] while ensuring the protection of trade secrets.

While the obligations stated in Article 13.4(d) of the Convention regarding disclosure of expenditures by the tobacco industry on advertising, promotion and sponsorship that is not yet prohibited apply only to Parties that do not have a comprehensive ban, all Parties should implement the recommended measures in line with Article 13.5, which encourages Parties to implement measures beyond their obligations under Article 13.4. Requiring disclosure by the tobacco industry of expenditures on all advertising, promotion and sponsorship in which it engages may help Parties that consider that they have a comprehensive ban to identify any advertising, promotion or sponsorship not covered by the ban or engaged in by the tobacco industry in contravention of the ban. Disclosure requirements may have the added benefit of discouraging the tobacco industry from engaging in tobacco advertising, promotion or sponsorship in which it might otherwise engage.

Recommendation

Parties should meet the requirements of Article 13.4 of the Convention regarding any form of tobacco advertising, promotion or sponsorship that is not prohibited. Parties should prohibit all promotion of a tobacco product by any means that are false, misleading, deceptive or likely to create an erroneous impression; mandate health or other appropriate warnings or messages; and require regular disclosure by the tobacco industry to authorities of any advertising, promotion and sponsorship in which it engages. Parties should make the disclosed information readily available to the public.

---

[9] This provision supports the obligation under Article 12(c) to promote public access to a wide range of information on the tobacco industry as relevant to the objectives of the Convention.

CONSISTENCY

Domestic bans and their effective enforcement are the cornerstones of any meaningful comprehensive ban on tobacco advertising, promotion and sponsorship at the global level. Contemporary media platforms such as the Internet, films and direct broadcast satellite easily cross borders, and many forms of advertising, promotion and sponsorship regulated by domestic rules, such as event sponsorship, are broadcast and disseminated widely to other States. Moreover, advertising and promotion are often linked to products such as items of clothing and technological devices or appear in publications, and thus move from one State to another when these items move.

It is obvious that the effectiveness of domestic bans can be undermined unless there is international cooperation.

Cross-border advertising, promotion and sponsorship originating from a Party's territory (out-flowing material)

Article 13.2 of the Convention states that "a comprehensive ban shall include, subject to the legal environment and technical means available to [each] Party, a comprehensive ban on cross-border advertising, promotion and sponsorship *originating from its territory*".

Implementation of the ban should cover, for example, all publications and products printed or produced within the territory of a Party, whether they are targeting persons within the Party's territory or persons in the territories of other States. It is often difficult to differentiate between publications or products targeting or actually used in the originating State and those targeting and used in other States.

The ban should also apply to the placing of tobacco advertising, promotion and sponsorship on the Internet or another cross-border communications technology by any person or entity within the territory of a Party, whether the material is targeting persons outside or inside that Party's territory.

Moreover, the ban should also apply to any person or entity that broadcasts tobacco advertising, promotion and sponsorship that could be received in another State.

A comprehensive ban on advertising, promotion and sponsorship originating from a Party's territory should also ensure that a Party's nationals – natural persons or legal persons – do not engage in advertising, promotion or sponsorship in the territory of another State, irrespective of whether it is imported back to their State of origin.

Cross-border advertising, promotion and sponsorship entering a Party's territory

Article 13.7 of the Convention states that "Parties which have a ban on certain forms of tobacco advertising, promotion and sponsorship have the sovereign right to ban those forms of cross-border tobacco advertising, promotion and sponsorship entering their territory and to impose equal penalties as those applicable to domestic advertising, promotion and sponsorship originating from their territory in accordance with their national law".

Implementation of the ban should cover, for example, publications and products printed or produced in other States entering the territory of a Party or targeting persons in that territory. Parties should consider carrying out sampling checks for imported consignments of printed publications. If such publications are printed, published or distributed by nationals of a Party or by entities established in a Party's territory, they should be held liable and the ban should be enforced to the fullest extent possible.[10] The ban should also apply to all Internet content that is accessible within a Party's territory and to any other audio, visual or audiovisual material broadcast into or otherwise received in a Party's territory, whether or not it is targeting persons in the territory of that Party.

Recommendations

Parties with a comprehensive ban or restrictions on tobacco advertising, promotion and sponsorship should ensure that any cross-border tobacco advertising, promotion and sponsorship originating from their territory is banned or restricted in the same manner as domestic tobacco advertising, promotion and sponsorship. Parties should make use of their sovereign right to take effective actions to limit or prevent any cross-border tobacco advertising, promotion and sponsorship entering their territory, whether from Parties that have restrictions or from non-Parties, recognizing that in some cases effective actions might have to be addressed in a protocol.

RESPONSIBLE ENTITIES

The responsible entities should be defined widely, covering the entire marketing chain. Primary responsibility should lie with the initiator of advertising, promotion or sponsorship, usually tobacco manufacturers, wholesale distributors, importers, retailers and their agents and associations.

Moreover, many other entities are involved in tobacco advertising, promotion and sponsorship and should also be held responsible.

Responsibility cannot be attributed in the same manner to all entities as their involvement in the production, placement and dissemination of tobacco

---

[10] A Party may also enforce its ban against non-nationals in some circumstances. How to address nationals of other Parties may be the subject of provisions of a possible protocol on cross-border advertising, promotion and sponsorship.

advertising, promotion and sponsorship varies. In the case of tobacco sponsorship, the responsible entities are those that make any relevant form of contribution, those that receive any relevant form of contribution and any intermediaries that facilitate the making or receiving of any relevant form of contribution. When tobacco advertising and promotion involve communication, the way in which entities should be held responsible depends on their role in the production and dissemination of the content of the communication and the possibilities they have to control it. The disseminator should be made responsible in so far as it is aware of, or was in a position to become aware of, the content of the advertising and promotion. This is true for whatever media or communications technology is involved, but it applies especially to controlling content on the Internet and disseminated via direct broadcast satellite.

In relation to all forms of media and communications:

- Persons or entities that produce or publish content (e.g. advertising agencies, designers, publishers of newspapers and other printed materials, broadcasters and producers of films, television and radio programmes, games and live performances, and Internet, mobile phone, satellite and game content producers) should be banned from including tobacco advertising, promotion and sponsorship.
- Persons or entities such as media and events organizers, sportspeople, celebrities, film stars and other artists should be banned from engaging in tobacco advertising, promotion and sponsorship.
- Particular obligations (for example, remove or disable access to content) should be applied to other entities involved in analogue or digital media and communication (such as social networking sites, Internet service providers and telecommunication companies), once they have been made aware of tobacco advertising, promotion and sponsorship.

In the case of legal entities, the responsibility should normally lie with the company, not with an individual employee.

A contract, agreement or arrangement concerning tobacco advertising, promotion or sponsorship should be held invalid if it is agreed in violation of a comprehensive ban.

In relation to the Internet, for example, there are five principal categories of responsible entity upon which bans or particular obligations should be imposed.

- *Content producers* create the content or cause it to be created. These include tobacco companies, advertising agencies and producers of television programmes, films and games that are distributed online. Content producers should be *banned* from including tobacco advertising, promotion or sponsorship in the content they produce.

- *Content publishers* include publishers and entities that select content before it is made available to Internet users (e.g. Internet sites of newspapers or broadcasters). Content publishers should be *banned* from including tobacco advertising, promotion or sponsorship in the content they make available.

- *Content hosts* are entities that control Internet-connected computer servers on which content is stored, including entities that aggregate content produced by others without selecting the content before they make it available to Internet users (such as social networking Internet sites). Content hosts should have an *obligation to remove or disable access to* tobacco advertising, promotion and sponsorship *once they have been made aware of the content.*

- *Content navigators* are entities, such as Internet search engines, that facilitate the location of content by users of communications services. Content navigators should have an *obligation to disable access to* tobacco advertising, promotion and sponsorship *once they have been made aware of the content.*

- *Access providers* are entities that provide end-user access to communications services, such as Internet service providers and mobile telephone companies. Access providers should have an *obligation to disable access to* tobacco advertising, promotion and sponsorship *once they have been made aware of the content.*

Unlike the obligations on content producers, content publishers and content hosts, Parties could limit the obligations on content navigators and access providers to using reasonable efforts to disable access in light of what is technically possible.

Recommendation

The entities responsible for tobacco advertising, promotion and sponsorship should be defined widely, and the way in which they are held responsible should depend on their role.

Primary responsibility should lie with the initiator of advertising, promotion or sponsorship, usually tobacco manufacturers, wholesale distributors, importers, retailers and their agents and associations.

Persons or entities that produce or publish media content should be banned from including tobacco advertising, promotion and sponsorship in the content they produce or publish.

Persons or entities (such as events organizers, sportspeople and celebrities) should be banned from engaging in tobacco advertising, promotion and sponsorship.

Particular obligations, for example, to remove content should be applied to other entities involved in analogue or digital media after they have been made aware of the tobacco advertising, promotion and sponsorship.

DOMESCTIC ENFORCEMENT OF LAWS ON TOBACCO ADVERTISING, PROMOTION AND SPONSORSHIP

Sanctions

Parties should introduce and apply effective, proportionate and dissuasive penalties (including fines, corrective advertising remedies and licence suspension or cancellation). In order that the penalties imposed be effective deterrents they should be graded and commensurate with the nature and seriousness of the offence(s), including a first offence, and should outweigh the potential economic benefits to be derived from the advertising, promotion or sponsorship.

Repeat infringements should incur a highly significant penalty for a manufacturer or responsible entity. In the case of frequent or flagrant infringements, more stringent sanctions should be imposed, including possible imprisonment. Sanctions should also include the obligation to remedy the infringement, for example by:

- removal of the advertising, promotion or sponsorship;
- publication of court decisions in a manner to be determined by the court and at the expense of the party or parties designated by the court; and
- funding of corrective or counter-advertising.

Sanctions should be applied to the conduct of entities and not only to individuals (including corporate entities that can be held responsible for the conduct of related corporate entities outside the territory but with an effect within the territory). Sanctions should also be applied to the conduct of managers, directors, officers and/or legal representatives of corporate entities when those individuals bear responsibility for the corporate entity's conduct.

Licensing of tobacco manufacturers, wholesale distributors, importers and retailers can be an effective method for controlling advertising, promotion and sponsorship. A licence would be granted or renewed only if the applicant could ensure compliance with the legal requirements. In cases of non-compliance, the licence could be withdrawn for a certain time or cancelled. For responsible entities not directly involved in producing or selling tobacco (such as broadcasters) when such entities are required to be licensed, compliance with the provisions on tobacco advertising, promotion and sponsorship should be included in the criteria for granting, renewing, suspending or revoking a licence.

If deterrent sanctions are in place, enforcement authorities might be successful in putting an end to illegal practices without court proceedings (e.g. by contacts, meetings, warnings, administrative decisions and periodic penalty payments).

Monitoring, enforcement and access to justice

Parties should designate a competent, independent authority to monitor and enforce the laws and entrust it with the necessary powers and resources. This agency should have the power to investigate complaints, seize unlawful advertising or promotion, and pronounce on complaints and/or initiate appropriate legal proceedings.

Civil society and citizens should be involved in the monitoring and effective enforcement of the ban. Civil society organizations, notably entities such as public health, health care, prevention, youth protection or consumer organizations, can be expected to undertake rigorous monitoring, and legislation should specify that members of the public may initiate complaints.

In addition, civil law options should be made available to oppose tobacco advertising, promotion and sponsorship. National law should enable any interested person or nongovernmental organization to initiate legal action against illegal tobacco advertising, promotion and sponsorship.

The enforcement programme may include a toll-free telephone complaint hotline, an Internet web site or a similar system to encourage the public to report violations.

Recommendation

Parties should introduce and apply effective, proportionate and dissuasive penalties. Parties should designate a competent, independent authority to monitor and enforce the law and entrust it with the necessary powers and resources. Civil society should be involved in the monitoring and enforcement of the law and have access to justice.

PUBLIC EDUCATION AND COMMUNITY AWARENESS

In the spirit of Article 12 of the Convention,[11] Parties should promote and strengthen public awareness of tobacco advertising, promotion and sponsorship in all sectors of society, using all available communication tools. Parties should, inter alia, adopt appropriate measures to promote broad access to effective, comprehensive public education and awareness programmes that underline the importance of a comprehensive ban, educate the public concerning its necessity and explain why advertising, promotion and sponsorship by the tobacco industry is unacceptable.

Engaging the support of the community to monitor compliance and report violations of laws against tobacco advertising, promotion and sponsorship is an essential element of enforcement. In order for members of the community to perform this role, they must be made aware of the problem and understand the law and the ways in which they can act on breaches.

---

[11] "Education, communication, training and public awareness".

Parties should implement public education and awareness programmes, inform members of the community about existing laws on tobacco advertising, promotion and sponsorship, the steps that can be taken to inform the relevant government agency of any advertising, promotion or sponsorship, and the steps that can be taken against a person who has engaged in tobacco advertising, promotion or sponsorship in breach of the law.

Recommendation

Parties should promote and strengthen, in all sectors of society, public awareness of the need to eliminate tobacco advertising, promotion and sponsorship, the laws against it, and the ways in which members of the public can act on breaches of these laws.

INTERNATIONAL COLLABORATION

The effectiveness of efforts to eliminate tobacco advertising, promotion and sponsorship depends not only on the initiatives undertaken by individual Parties but also on the extent to which Parties cooperate in addressing tobacco advertising, promotion and sponsorship. Effective international cooperation will be essential to the elimination of both domestic and cross-border tobacco advertising, promotion and sponsorship.

Parties to the Convention already have undertaken commitments with respect to international cooperation, including under Article 13.6 (*Cooperation in the development of technologies and other means necessary to facilitate the elimination of cross-border advertising*); Article 19 (*Liability*); Article 20 (*Research, surveillance and exchange of information*); particularly Article 20.4 (*Exchange of publicly available, scientific, technical, socioeconomic, commercial and legal information, as well as information regarding the practices of the tobacco industry*); Article 21 (*Reporting and exchange of information*); Article 22 (*Cooperation in the scientific, technical, and legal fields and provision of related expertise*); and Article 26 (*Financial resources*).

In addition to the recommendations in these guidelines, the Conference of the Parties also takes note of the recommendations of the working group on other measures with respect to facilitation of the exchange of information and other cooperation between Parties that would contribute to the elimination of cross-border advertising, promotion and sponsorship.[12] Such measures to eliminate domestic tobacco advertising, promotion or sponsorship are also beneficial, recognizing that Parties would benefit from sharing information, experience and expertise in respect of *all* tobacco advertising, promotion and sponsorship, not only cross-border tobacco advertising, promotion and sponsorship.

---

[12] Decision FCTC/COP3(14)

APPENDIX

Indicative (non-exhaustive) list of forms of tobacco advertising, promotion and sponsorship within the terms of the Convention

- communication through audio, visual or audiovisual means: print (including newspapers, magazines, pamphlets, leaflets, flyers, letters, billboards, posters, signs), television and radio (including terrestrial and satellite), films, DVDs, videos and CDs, games (computer games, video games or online games), other digital communication platforms (including the Internet and mobile phones) and theatre or other live performance;
- brand-marking, including in entertainment venues and retail outlets and on vehicles and equipment (e.g. by use of brand colours or schemes of colours, logos or trademarks);
- display of tobacco products at points of sale;
- tobacco product vending machines;
- Internet sales of tobacco products;
- brand stretching and brand sharing (product diversification);
- product placement (i.e. the inclusion of, or reference to, a tobacco product, service or trademark in the context of communication (see above), in return for payment or other consideration);
- provision of gifts or discounted products with the purchase of tobacco products (e.g. key rings, T-shirts, baseball hats, cigarette lighters);
- supply of free samples of tobacco products, including in conjunction with marketing surveys and taste testing;
- incentive promotions or loyalty schemes, e.g. redeemable coupons provided with purchase of tobacco products;
- competitions, associated with tobacco products or brand names, whether requiring the purchase of a tobacco product or not;
- direct targeting of individuals with promotional (including informational) material, such as direct mail, telemarketing, "consumer surveys" or "research";
- promotion of discounted products;
- sale or supply of toys or sweets that resemble tobacco products;
- payments or other contributions to retailers to encourage or induce them to sell products, including retailer incentive programmes (e.g. rewards to retailers for achieving certain sales volumes);
- packaging and product design features;
- payment or other consideration in exchange for the exclusive sale or prominent display of a particular product or particular manufacturer's product in a retail outlet, at a venue or at an event;
- sale, supply, placement and display of products at educational establishments or at hospitality, sporting, entertainment, music, dance and social venues or events;

ARTICLE 13

- provision of financial or other support to events, activities, individuals or groups (such as sporting or arts events, individual sportspeople or teams, individual artists or artistic groups, welfare organizations, politicians, political candidates or political parties), whether or not in exchange for publicity, including corporate social responsibility activities; and

- provision of financial or other support by the tobacco industry to venue operators (such as pubs, clubs or other recreational venues) in exchange for building or renovating premises to promote tobacco products or the use or provision of awnings and sunshades.